RESEARCH HIGHLIGHTS IN SOCIAL WORK 32

Social Care and Housing

Edited by Ian Shaw, Susan Lambert and David Clapham

Jessica Kingsley Publishers
London and Philadelphia

Research Highlights in Social Work 32
Editors: Ian Shaw, Susan Lambert and David Clapham
Secretary: Anne Forbes
Editorial Advisory Committee:

Professor J. Lishman	Robert Gordon University, Aberdeen
Ms M. Buist	Independent Researcher, Edinburgh
Mr P. Cassidy	Social Work Department, Aberdeen City Council, representing the Association of Directors of Social Work
Ms A. Connor	Lothian Health, Edinburgh
Mr D. Cox	Robert Gordon University, Aberdeen
Mr M. King	Northern College, Aberdeen
Dr F. Paterson	Social Work Services Group, Scottish Office
Ms C. Smith	Scottish Council for Voluntary Organisations, Edinburgh
Dr A. Robertson	University of Edinburgh

Robert Gordon University
School of Applied Social Studies
Kepplestone Annexe, Queen's Road
Aberdeen AB15 4PH

First published in 1998 by
Jessica Kingsley Publishers Ltd
116 Pentonville Road
London N1 9JB, England
and
325 Chestnut Street
Philadelphia, PA 19106, USA

Copyright © 1998 Robert Gordon University, Research Highlights Advisory Group, School of Applied Social Studies

Library of Congress Cataloguing in Publication Data
A CIP catalogue record for this book is available from the Library of Congress
British Library Cataloguing in Publication Data
Social work and housing. - (Research highlights in social work; 32) 1. Social service - Great Britain 2. Housing - Great Britain 3. Housing management - Great Britain 4. Social work with the homeless - Great Britain I. Title II. Clapham, David
363.5'1'0941

ISBN 185302 437 6

Printed and Bound in Great Britain by
Athenaeum Press, Gateshead, Tyne and Wear

RESEARCH HIGHLIGHTS IN SOCIAL WORK 32

Social Care and Housing

Research Highlights in Social Work Series

This topical series of books examines areas currently of particular interest to those in community work and related fields. Each book draws together a collection of articles on different aspects of the subject under discussion highlighting relevant research and drawing out implications for policy and practice. The project is under the general direction of Professor Joyce Lishman.

Contents

List of tables

CHAPTER 1

Boundaries of Change in Social Care and Housing

Ian Shaw, Susan Lambert and David Clapham

Social workers' hold on the significance of housing issues is weak. This weakness is apparent on three counts. First, social work interest is restricted to issues of special needs and acute problems of housing malaise such as overcrowding or homelessness, with the result that solutions to the problems facing service users tend to be limited to the application of existing resources. Second, there is a lack of analytical backbone in the strategies of both practitioners and social work educators. This is partly due to the way in which housing research and welfare research are both marginalised within the social sciences. Third, there is a recurrent tendency on the part of social workers to declining engagement in and withdrawal from housing issues. Indeed, it is not unreasonable to conclude that the relationship between social work and housing, far from becoming more closely integrated, is in decline. The short-lived advocacy of community social work in the early 1980s following the publication of the Barclay report and the earlier vigour of community development in the previous decade both sustained a central role for housing issues within the social work task, but they have long since slipped below the horizon.

The contributors to this book will develop two broad solutions to these problems. First, social care requires practice which is rooted in an analysis of broader social problems and which invites social workers to connect the problems facing citizens and users of services with structural issues of poverty, race, gender, health, employment and education. Second, the solution rests in the promotion of social work interventions in housing and social care practice which are wider than attempts to find resources to meet special needs.

There is a troubled social and economic context for practice of this kind. Social inequalities are wide and increasing in Britain. The share of income received by the richest and the poorest households has steadily widened from the mid 1970s. Average real incomes may have increased over the same period but the lower income groups have not shared in this increase. Income trends suggest an increasingly polarised society. These inequalities find their reflection in the population's levels of health and education. Infant mortality rates, chronic respiratory illness, disability, dietary standards and death rates all demonstrate the relative disadvantage of low income individuals and families. The link between education and social background has been repeatedly demonstrated. Employment opportunities, housing conditions, and environmental disadvantage all depress educational performance.

Housing trends are a key element in these patterns of inequality. The 1950s and 1960s were marked by a period of inclusionary housing policy in Britain, when the suburbs expanded and direct state provision of housing as a social right was accepted. These policies were not without problems, for example they elevated the citizenship of white male industrial workers and were premised on the partial citizenship of women and ethnic minorities. However, the wider resurgence of inequality has led to the polarisations in income, education and health being reflected in social divisions in housing tenure. Tenants of council housing have increasingly been made up of households in the lowest income groups and in receipt of means-tested benefits. While this residualisation process was well established before the 1980s, it has continued throughout the subsequent years, and applies to tenants in both council housing and housing associations. This has led to 'satiated elites and deprived minorities' (Forrest and Kennett 1994, p.135) with these minorities concentrated in means tested, targeted and marginalised forms of housing.

> The pattern is one of cumulative and persistent deprivation
> which affects health, education and job opportunities, and
> prolongs and deepens disadvantage so far that it handicaps
> particular sections of the community and reduces opportunities
> and choices...Polarisation between housing tenures...has meant
> that those with the lowest incomes are being concentrated in the

social rented sector and in particular neighbourhoods.
(Lee, Murie, Marsh and Riseborough, 1995 p.12)

Problems shot through with issues of housing and shelter are part of the day-to-day work of social workers, whether this be with young people leaving care, offenders, people with disabilities or mental health problems, those with drug or alcohol related problems, older people facing physical frailty or the onset of dementia, women at risk of domestic violence, or carers needing respite from the daily grind of caring. The headlines selected almost at random from the housing and national press during 1997 shout the housing problems of those who are likely to come into contact with social workers:

Neighbours make life Hell for HIV Sufferers.
Paedophile Outed by Police and Probation.
Ethnic Minority Elders Lack Sensitive Support.
People at Risk Swell Homeless Numbers.
Problem Drinkers need Prompt Help and Home.
More Women are Sleeping on the Streets.
Benefit Changes Push Refugees onto Streets.

In the chapters that follow the contributors address *analytical frameworks* for understanding the relationship between housing and social care, *strategies* for formulating coherent responses, and ways of improving *service delivery* and *social work practice*. We are aware that we need to take the proposals further than we have found possible in this book. The research on which we have drawn is itself lopsided in the attention that has been given to different aspects of the relationship between social care and housing and it is possible that we have been insufficiently sharp in elucidating the implications of research that has been completed. Yet we have undertaken this book because we believe that there is now, perhaps for the first time, a strong body of practice-relevant research which allows a fresh analytic perspective on one of the chronic weaknesses of social welfare.

During the 1990s housing researchers have shown far more interest than social work researchers in the boundaries between social care and housing. There have been dozens of such research studies since 1990, and it is these studies which sustain the analysis and recommendations for good social work practice in this book.

However, the conclusions drawn from such research are not overly optimistic. For example, the implementation of an allegedly needs-led community care provision has been followed by well-grounded fears that people encounter problems in relation to the assessment of their needs, the provision of information, and the planning and management of their needs. For example, recent research shows that older people are not encouraged to articulate needs and wishes that cannot be provided for, and if they express a need that cannot be provided for then it is rarely recorded (Midgley, Munlo and Brown 1997). The result is that the system is not properly open to scrutiny and the needs and wishes of people remain invisible to planners. Agency-based assessments do not meet the hidden needs of people in the community who are not in touch with agencies. Holistic, multi-agency planning for older people simply does not take place. Most services are offered in a pre-packaged form that does not allow the flexibility and choice that users say they need.

Homelessness experience and research is no more sanguine. John Bird, the driving force behind *The Big Issue,* has vigorously criticised British homelessness agencies from the conference platform for being territorial, predatory and competitive, and for lacking overall perspective, and unnecessarily multiplying agencies. Similar complaints have been heard about European agencies, and Rossi has bemoaned 'the rancorous politics of homelessness' in America (Rossi 1987).

This dissonance between aspiration and achievement makes it timely to review research and experience—to consolidate recent practice and research, and to set the agenda for the future. In a previous analysis of social work and housing the Stewarts suggested three appropriate and achievable objectives for those who write books for practitioners.

> First, to alert the reader to the dimensions of an issue; prompting relevant questions to ask, and where to seek answers. Secondly, to suggest criteria for formulating strategies towards some kind of solution...Thirdly, building practitioners' confidence on the basis of information about what others have been able to achieve in similar situations. (Stewart and Stewart, 1992 p.25)

This movement from analysis to practice is echoed in the following chapters. Social workers have most often viewed housing issues as a problem of securing the most appropriate resource to address the special needs of social work service users. While special needs provision is addressed in this book (e.g. by Franklin in Chapter 9 and also as part of wider arguments by Wasoff and Chakrabarti in Chapters 7 and 8), the unifying concern is to rescue housing issues from their position of marginalisation within social work and, as Drakeford and Williamson conclude in Chapter 10, to lay the foundation for 'a reconnection of social workers with the social circumstances of their users'. Shaw and Stewart develop this reconnection through a consideration of housing poverty and of social exclusion (in Chapters 2 and 3). While there are sharp differences between contributors–compare for example, Allen (Chapter 5) and Oldman (Chapter 4) for their treatment of the boundaries between social work and housing professionals–we eschew the rhetoric of adversarial politics and professional imperialism, which has sometimes led to social workers and housing managers talking past each other. We also endeavour to combine lessons from research which has a strong analysis of organisational *process,* with inferences about organisational *structures* and training for practice (e.g. Wiseman and Hayton in Chapter 6).

In this introductory survey we sketch the wider economic, political and social trends which impinge on social work and housing, both in the United Kingdom and Europe, and lead from there to an outline of those developments and trends within housing which have special relevance to social work. This introduction also provides the context for the following chapter, in which the contributions to this book are located in relation to the questions facing social work and housing at the turn of the new century.

The contexts for housing and social care

Social workers have tended to concentrate entirely on arguments regarding public housing, perhaps assuming that the broader patterns of demography and home ownership have less relevance for those with and for whom they work. Throughout Europe there have been demographic changes which affect housing and in turn social work. There has been an expansion of home ownership, a marginalisation of social housing, and a growth in homelessness. It is sometimes claimed that there has been an increase in the number of dwellings available and that therefore the housing shortage is now less acute. There is a potential fallacy in this argument. For example, the number of dwellings per 1000 people has risen from 300 per 1000 people in Britain at the mid century point to 400 per 1000 people at the time of the 1991 census - an apparent one-third increase in the availability of dwellings.

However, over the same period the size of the average household has fallen from 3.3 people to 2.5 people. Therefore we cannot conclude that there are now more dwellings available *per household*.

It is a familiar fact that growth in prosperity has not been spread equitably across the social canvas. There has been a growth of 'work rich' and 'work poor' families. It is a startling fact that 60 per cent of women with husbands in work are also in work, whereas of women whose husbands are not in work only 24 per cent are in work. There have emerged fears of an 'underclass' fed by tabloid stories of single mothers bringing up families in longterm dependence on state benefits. The evidence in support of such conclusions is far from straightforward. Shaw and Stewart both explore ways in which the language of underclass may be a rhetoric to disguise racism. Fears have been expressed that governments may have been searching for a language for giving up on poor people.

A cluster of trends regarding the marketisation of housing and welfare, the culture of quality, the Citizen's Charter, and views about citizenship are also part of the context for social care and housing. The application of market ideas has repeatedly been criticised as being of limited applicability to welfare (e.g. Fitzgeorge-Butler and Williams 1995; Kirkpatrick and Lucio 1995; Pfeffer and Coote 1991). Managing, monitoring and rewarding quality often lead to uniformity, rigidity and monotony, rather than diversity. Standards and norms can become stereotypes which create rather than resolve problems. Restricted opportunities for participation limit the opportunity for criticism ('voice'), while power differentials and service monopolies make impossible the exercise of alternative service choices ('exit'). When exit and voice options are not available it is possible that service users will engage in withdrawal and retreat ('flight') from services. The underlying point here is that there is a close link between social exclusion and citizenship. Housing exclusion leads to citizenship exclusion. Citizenship is both a set of *rights* (who is entitled to become a citizen?) and a *process* of active citizenship. Exclusion from housing is a loss of active citizenship (Blanc 1994).

Social workers have also been concerned with potential threats to citizenship as a set of rights. The Housing Act, 1996 and the Asylum and Immigration Act, 1996 removed local authorities' duty to assist asylum seekers, thus in effect severely restricting asylum seekers' eligibility for income support, housing and council tax benefits. The Court of Appeal ruled that these regulations were *ultra vires*, and they were withdrawn when the Court of Appeal also ruled that destitute asylum seekers are vulnerable and in 'priority need' under the homelessness legislation. The debate continued into 1997 when the Council for Racial Equality criticised the Housing Corporation as potentially discriminatory in its position over housing asylum seekers. There are approximately 36,000 asylum seekers annually, with figures in the housing trade press revealing that in London alone over 7000 asylum seekers were refused permanent housing and benefits in the early months of 1997.

The incoming Labour government of 1997 made a Manifesto promise regarding the private rented sector, to introduce a licensing system which would benefit tenants and responsible landlords. The government also planned to introduce a new housing tenure, 'commonhold', to enable people living in flats to own their own homes individually and to own the whole building collectively. There were widely signalled intentions to use capital receipts from the sale of council houses for the re-investment in new homes and rehabilitation of old ones. In the field of homelessness Labour promised to introduce a duty on local authorities to protect those who are homeless through no fault of their own and are in priority need. They also signalled a plan to support a push to promote energy conservation by the support of home energy schemes.

There are positive features to these policies. Higher standards of energy efficiency are certainly needed. The housing stock in Britain has very low levels of energy efficiency and it is estimated that between 30,000 and 60,000 people die each year because of inadequately heated homes. The higher profile for homelessness was also welcome, although a serious failing was that no targets were set for the number of homes to be built. Under present levels of investment there will be 42,000 new homes in 1999, the lowest since the Second World War. The previous Conservative government estimated that there will be 4.4 million new households formed by 2016, but no party has a clear policy for where they will live. Dependence on market forces for private house-building is also likely to worsen the growing threat to greenfield sites hitherto protected under greenbelt policies. The Labour government made some valuable promises to improve the *processes* by which housing is delivered, maintained, and regulated, but promised far less about the level of *outputs*.

Developments in housing and social care within the United Kingdom are shaped not only by political and social trends in Britain, but increasingly by trends in other European member states. Housing agencies in Britain have become gradually more sensitive to the implications of policies developed at the level of the European Commission (EC), and their impact on housing and social work policies in member states. A well-known limit to European Union (EU) activities in the housing sector is that the Treaty of Rome (1957) and the Single European Act (1985) contain no reference to housing or living conditions. This lack of legal competence is held in association with the principle of subsidiarity, under which European Commission action cannot be substituted for actions undertaken at member state level, but must complement them.

Social housing and the European Union

However, there is a series of wider EC policy remits enabling research and action to be taken which can tackle social and housing problems. There are 'budgetlines' such as the European Regional Development Fund, the European Social Fund, and the Community Initiatives which are intended to close the gap between the economic prosperity of the advanced and less developed regions in the Union. Access is not easy because budgetary procedures vary widely from one department to another, and most of the departments of the Commission do not publish guidelines explaining the selection criteria. The best practice for social work and social housing agencies wishing to apply for European funding is to look for partners, and ensure that proposals are defined in EC terms (e.g. by not making housing the principal objective).

There are several programmes which are relevant to social workers. The Community Initiatives programme (1994–1999) includes funding to increase access to the employment market for those threatened with exclusion (Horizon), funds to encourage integration into the labour market of young people under 20 (Youthstart), and schemes for depressed urban areas (URBAN). The Action Programme to Combat Poverty and Social Exclusion, measures to benefit the free movement of workers, measures for elderly persons, community measures for disabled persons, and energy and environment programmes all have potential for exploiting the underlying housing dimensions of welfare problems.

Social exclusion has been a major aim of social policy in other countries of the European Union and also in central and eastern Europe. Social exclusion - the process through which individuals or groups are partially or wholly excluded from participation in their society - brings together both fiscal and welfare measures, and has its legislative basis in the Maastricht Treaty, and in particular the Social Chapter. Following the British government becoming a signatory to the Social Chapter, it is likely that there will be growing discussion of the role of social workers in combating social exclusion, and increasing interest in the revival of a broader community role for social workers. Such a role is likely to bring positive consequences for engaging in action at the borders of welfare and housing. These developments are not restricted to EU member states.

> As these developments have been taking place in the EU, in Central and Eastern Europe the emphasis has been on what is called the Civil Society. Following the collapse of the centralised welfare bureaucracies of the Communist years, the individual's relationship with the State is being redefined from one of subjection to Party organisations, to one of free association through involvement in...a huge diversity of community-based groups. (National Institute for Social Work 1996)

Different traditions for the provision of housing, the absence of a housing profession in much of Europe, different national research traditions, political rivalries between housing agencies, and the varying impacts in different parts of Europe of wider social trends such as East/West migration, all make it difficult to envisage a European position on social work and housing. The European Federation of National Organisations Working with the Homeless (FEANTSA) based in Brussels, the European Liaison Committee for Social Housing (CECODHAS), and the European Network for Housing Research work to alert European institutions and national governments to the need to alleviate and eliminate homelessness in the case of FEANTSA, and provide networks for agencies and researchers. The National Institute for Social Work has taken a lead among British organisations in opening up the implications of European policy and research carried out in this field.

Housing trends

This section outlines five key themes in housing chosen because of their particular impact on the quality of life of social work clients: housing need, access to housing, homelessness, condition of housing and housing finance and affordability.

Housing need is pivotal to an understanding of these five themes. The extent of housing need will be assessed, followed by an appraisal of the causes of this pressing social problem. In this way we will address some of the issues that confront social workers in their daily routine. Housing policy has been predicated in the main on the needs of family groups and this emphasis necessarily excludes a large group of single young people who have experienced homelessness or poor quality housing in disproportionate numbers. Policy shifts since the 1980s have seen an expansion of the owner-occupied sector, including the sale of council housing, which has taken place at the expense of social rented housing. The phrase 'social' housing is used to include housing built with government subsidy and rented from not-for-profit organisations like local authorities and housing associations. Privatisation policies mean that housing associations that are not strictly in the public sector, but are the key providers of new build homes for rent, have been forced to borrow an increased amount from private lenders to develop new homes. This has had the effect of pushing up rents in this sector, although they may not be as high as local authority rents in some areas. The private rented sector, to which more families in need have been pushed since the 1996 Housing Act came into force, is characterised by high rents and rundown housing.

Housing need

Research highlights a continuing need for investment in social housing, and a shortage of suitable accommodation. During the 1990s construction of social rented housing in England and Wales fell far below estimated levels of need with 1994/95, seeing the lowest level of combined housing association and local authority starts since 1945 (Coulter 1996). About 30,000 more homes a year should have been built between 1991 and 1995 to meet estimated demand. Studies predict that demand for low-priced rented accommodation in England will amount to 1.3m homes to the year 2011 (Holmans 1995). In a further study in Wales Holmans (1996) estimated that demand for new rented homes would average between 4000 and 5000 homes a year from 1991 to 2001 and 5000 a year in the following decade. At current levels of building the backlog of unmet need will be 400,000 in England and 25,000 homes in Wales by 2001.

Most of the new demand for housing will be for homes in the public rented sector. The demand for owner occupied housing is shrinking as the demand for low cost rented homes is growing. The rate of increase in demand for owner occupation is predicted to be 3 per cent annually up to 2011 (Holmans 1995). Half the total demand for new homes will come from adults born during the baby boom years of the late 1970s and early 1980s and single people, those who remain single by choice, but also people experiencing relationship breakdown.

Accommodation to meet the housing needs of women and children escaping domestic violence is also far from adequate (Charles 1994; Malos and Hague 1993). In a study in Wales Charles found that the shortage of refuges and move-on accommodation meant that women either had to return to abusive partners or to stay for long periods in temporary housing. This meant fewer crisis places were available for other women in need of safety. Those refuges that do exist face doubts about funding, (Malos and Hague 1993).

Access to housing

Policy in recent years has had the effect of expanding owner occupation and helping the better-off. In 1979 35 per cent of British homes were in the social rented sector compared to around 25 per cent in 1996. The effect of changes in access to public housing is that the social and economic base of tenants is becoming narrower. About 72 per cent of new heads of household are people aged 16 to 29 years, compared to 14 per cent of existing tenants (Burrows 1997). New tenants are more likely to be out of work, or to be unable to work because they are single parents with young children. Households moving out of the social rented sector to become owner occupiers are likely to consist of couples, aged under 45 years and working. Those existing tenants who have been forced to remain in the sector tend to be older people living on pensions and other state benefits. A consequence of the narrowing social base of tenants in the social rented sector is that a significant proportion of children are disadvantaged. Twenty-five per cent of all children live in this sector where many adults are long-term unemployed, eligible for welfare benefits or have limited access to other community services like schools, health centres, leisure and cultural facilities.

A complex mix of central government and local housing policies and housing management practices produces a range of inequalities in access to housing and exacerbates the problem of housing need. Research shows that a wide range of factors lead to discrimination against applicants for housing on the basis of race, class, gender or sexual orientation (Smith 1989; Henderson and Karn 1987; Smailes 1994; see the contributions to this volume by Wasoff and Chakrabarti). Single parent families, homeless applicants and ethnic minority households are likely to be offered homes of the worst quality. Lesbian and gay couples are discriminated against because of harassment and lack of succession rights to private or local authority tenancies.

Homelessness

Inequalities in access to housing, as well as a variety of other structural social, political and economic factors can result in homelessness. Estimates of homelessness vary widely depending on which agency is collecting the figures and the methodology of estimation (Shaw, Bloor and Roberts 1996), but there has been a substantial increase in homelessness since the 1970s. Government figures of homelessness are based on those persons and families accepted as homeless by local authorities; there were 150,501 such homeless acceptances in 1994 (Lund 1996). However less conservative agencies estimate that 1,712,000 people were homeless in Britain in the early 1990s (Burrows and Walentowicz 1992). This latter figure also includes people sleeping rough, households with children and other individuals in temporary accommodation, split households, those involuntarily sharing housing and people due to be discharged from an institution. The 1977 Housing (Homeless Persons) Act, consolidated in the 1985 Housing Act, entitled certain homeless households to a permanent secure home. In order to be rehoused applicants had to be considered vulnerable or at risk. Having children meant that a household would be provided with a home as did vulnerability on the grounds of childhood or old age, pregnancy, mental illness or disability. Applicants also had to be unintentionally homeless and to have a local connection. Exceptions to this last rule were women escaping abuse by a partner. Domestic violence accounts for eleven per cent of homelessness acceptances in London, and 25 per cent in some boroughs (Burns 1997). However, Burns points out that one third of Shelter's domestic violence cases in London involve illegal or inadequate local authority practice, including refusal to offer applicants temporary or permanent housing.

The 1996 Housing Act was due to bring to an end the duty of local authorities to provide permanent homes for homeless households. The incoming 1997 Labour Government moved quickly to preserve some priority for homeless households in local authority allocation schemes by amending the 1996 Act in this regard and give a 'reasonable preference' to the homeless along with other kinds of housing need. Critics of the proposed legislation as first published in the 1994 Green Paper warned that the proposals contradicted the intention of the Children Act 1989 that families with children should be provided with a long-term and permanent home. Shelter argued that the proposals could mean disruption to home life every six or twelve months and would make a settled family life 'extremely difficult' (Shelter 1995). The Association of London Authorities (1994) pointed out that the proposals failed to recognise the importance of joint assessment by housing and social services departments set in place following the NHS and Community Care Act 1990. Nor did they offer any solution to resolve conflicting interpretations of duties under this Act or the 1989 Children Act.

Eligibility criteria to be accepted by local authorities as being in priority need of housing meant that very few single people were eligible for housing. Local authorities have a duty to house those people who were vulnerable due to old age, mental illness or learning difficulties, or people leaving prison or other long-stay institutions but have no obligation to house other single people.

Male single homelessness is a far more visible problem than female homelessness. In a survey of people in hostels and bed-and-breakfast hotels, day centres and using soup runs, 23 per cent, 7 per cent and 13 per cent, were women (Anderson, Kemp and Quilgars 1993). However, as Watson and Austerberry (1986) suggest, homelessness amongst single women tends to be experienced in private rather than in public. Single women are far less likely to be street homeless because of the associated risks of harassment, violence and rape (NFHA 1993).

Most local authorities with effective strategies to support single homeless men and women work with other agencies such as social services, probation, housing associations and other voluntary organisations (McClusky 1997). Joint working arrangements mean a number of benefits, including improved assessment of needs, better targeting of resources and improved services. In a study of English and Welsh housing authorities McClusky found a number of constructive initiatives including provision of new build and self-build housing, rent guarantee schemes and counselling services for tenants in difficulties with their tenancies. Triggers to some successful schemes to help single homeless people were the Children Act 1989 and

the NHS and Community Care Act. All local authorities had to establish joint assessment procedures under these Acts.

The Rough Sleepers Initiative pumped £96m into a solution to develop emergency hostel spaces and more permanent 'move on' accommodation for homeless
people in London. Between 1990-1994 the Department of the Environment
claimed to have reduced the numbers of people sleeping rough in central London
from between 1000 and 2000 to 290 (DoE 1995). The scheme was due to finish in
1993 but the government made available an additional £86 million to continue the
scheme for three years. The White Paper *Our Future Homes* (DoE/Welsh Office
1995) proposed extending the initiative to other major cities where homelessness
was considered 'a major problem.' In 1996 it was introduced in Bristol and Glasgow and the 1997 Labour government committed itself to further extensions of
this policy initiative.

House condition

Shelter estimates that there is a backlog of housing repairs in England and Wales
costing £20bn. Quality of housing may be measured in terms of fitness, state of repair, overcrowding and access to basic amenities like piped water, an indoor lava-
tory and access to mains drains. In the UK 1.6 million homes fail the 'fitness
standard' and are considered unfit for human habitation or, in Scotland, are below
the 'tolerable standard'. Homes in Wales are amongst the worst quality with 1 in 8
homes unfit, compared to 1 in 14 in the UK as a whole. Poor state of repair is also a
problem, with 1 in 5 homes in England needing urgent repairs valued at £1,000 or
more and in Scotland one tenth of all homes require repairs costing £3,000 or
more. Twenty-five per cent of homes in Northern Ireland are in need of repairs
costing £3,500. There are clear regional differences in unfitness with industrial
districts and cities in the Midlands and North and rural areas of Scotland having
the worst quality housing (Leather and Morrison 1997). People most likely to live
in poor housing conditions are people on low income. Household income is less
than £8,000 per year for 60 per cent of people living in unfit housing and 50 per
cent of people living in homes needing extensive repairs. The highest number of
poor quality homes are in the owner occupied sector, because there are more
homes in this sector in the UK than any other. However, the highest proportion of
rundown housing is in the private rented sector. Two in five private tenants live in

homes that are unfit or in need of urgent repairs. Poor quality homes are being replaced at horrifyingly low levels. From 1990-94 just 6700 unfit homes were replaced, compared to 90,000 a year during the early 1970s (Leather and Morrison 1997).

The 1989 Local Government and Housing Act introduced a new grant system for repairs and improvement in the owner occupied sector and since then the number of grants given annually has fallen significantly to 100,000 per year compared to three times that many in the early 1980s. However local councils, who are unable to build new housing, are renovating their homes at record levels: 300,000 of local authority homes were repaired in 1994.

The English House Condition Survey indicates that 3 per cent (517,000) of households live in overcrowded conditions (DoE 1993). Overcrowding is closely linked to poor mental and physical health, and low educational attainment of children. Psychological distress is increased amongst women living in overcrowded homes (Gabe and Williams 1989). It has been linked to high levels of fire and accidents in the home (Lowry 1991) and to psychological difficulties in childhood (Arblaster and Hawtin 1994).

Housing finance and affordability

A traditional aim of housing policy has been to provide good quality low-priced homes–'a decent home for every family at a price within their means' (HMSO 1977) and 'a decent home within the reach of every family' (DoE/Welsh Office 1995). Closer examination of policy in practice calls into question the extent to which these aims have been fully achieved. Very many vulnerable or at risk families and individuals have not had their need for a low-rent and cheap-to-run home met.

Those households which have managed to secure a home in the social rented sector may find their good fortune has been tempered over recent years by anxiety about the rising cost of their rent. Local authority tenants faced rent rises of up to 36 per cent in real terms between 1988/89 and 1993/94 and 51 per cent between 1979/80 and 1982/83–a time when sales of council houses peaked. In the housing association sector fair rents (for pre-1989 tenancies) rose by 27 per cent in real terms between 1989/90 and 1993/94 while assured rents (post 1988 tenancies) increased by 43 per cent (Newton 1994). Housing costs were forced up during the early part of the 1990s by reductions both in subsidies to local authorities, and in housing association grants. The 1988 Housing Act required associations to make up the funding shortfall caused by reductions in state grants to develop new homes by borrowing from banks and building societies. In 1979-80 68 per cent of state expenditure for housing costs was spent on 'bricks and mortar' subsidies and 10 per cent on means tested subsidies for householders. Fifteen years later 49 per cent of government support was spent on 'bricks and mortar' and 27 per cent on housing benefit.

The outcome has been affordability problems for both associations and their tenants. If rents are to be affordable from a landlord's perspective it inevitably means that they are not affordable for the majority of their tenants. Associations needed to charge rents that were affordable for them - in that they are high enough to produce rental income streams that were sufficient to build up reserves that would make them attractive to private lenders. Future rental income streams were an important asset upon which banks and buildings societies placed great emphasis (Chaplin *et al.* 1995). But rents that may have brought comfort to associations inevitably meant discomfort for their tenants. Since 1988 rents have risen by as much as 12 per cent per annum and many tenants have become caught in the poverty trap. The depth of the poverty trap has been exacerbated by the replacement of the 'bricks and mortar' subsidies to develop new housing for rent with personal subsidies or means-tested housing benefit. Working tenants with high incomes left the rented sector for owner occupation and tax relief on mortgage payments leaving low-income tenants and those people on benefits to face higher rents. More low-income working tenants became dependent on housing benefits and those with children depended on family credit to make up low wages from paid work. Poor levels of pay in a deregulated labour market meant that many tenants became ensnared in a benefits trap: rents were only affordable if low wages were topped up by housing benefit or family credit. However the commitment to work of most tenants was strong, indeed many tenants took jobs even though they would be financially better off on benefits (Ford, Kempson and England, 1996).

The net result of a decade of conflicting housing and social security policy is a real policy muddle with rents driven up by the costs of developing new homes and expenditure on welfare benefits driven up by rents. Overall the total real cost to the taxpayer of social housing, including capital and revenue expenditure and housing benefit, has stayed the same at about £13.8 billion between 1980/81 and 1992/93 at 1991/92 prices (Hills 1993). The highest price has been paid by tenants themselves trapped by high rents and dependency on housing benefit.

Supported housing

Some people have needs both for housing and for some form of care or support. Housing agencies have responded to this mixture of needs in a number of ways, but the predominant approach has been through the provision of supported accommodation in which housing and support are integrated and provided as a, usually fixed, package. The most plentiful form of this is sheltered housing which was particularly popular in the 1960s and 1970s when it was seen as a panacea for the needs of a population which is growing older. Peter Townsend in 1962 urged the expansion of sheltered housing as an alternative to residential care which he argued could be phased out completely (Townsend 1962).

Sheltered housing offered older people support in a homely setting which fostered independence, but it never completely replaced residential care. During the 1980s a debate emerged over the efficacy of sheltered housing and increasing criticism focused on the rigidity of the models adopted and who benefited from it (Butler, Oldman and Greve 1983). The research showed that most older people entered schemes because of the small, modern, easily managed housing and some of the facilities were used by only a few of the tenants. In particular the wardens found themselves largely helping the frailer tenants and if there were too many of these in any scheme the staff were overwhelmed (Clapham and Munro 1990).

The reaction to these criticisms and problems was mixed. In some cases the support provided was upgraded and 'very sheltered' or 'extra care' housing created. In others attempts were made to make the provision more flexible by opening out the facilities to older people living nearby and using the schemes as a base for domiciliary carers. Alternatives such as community alarm systems, care and repair schemes and aids and adaptations were devised as a way of helping older people to stay in their own homes and although there are major problems of funding with each of these they have collectively reduced the demand for sheltered housing. Increasingly many landlords are now finding that some of their less popular schemes are becoming difficult to let. Problems have also arisen in financing the running costs of schemes which have usually been recouped through service charges which can be met by housing benefit. There have been repeated government and judicial attempts to restrict the scope of housing benefit which would threaten the financial viability of many supported accommodation schemes.

Supported accommodation has been developed to meet a wide range of needs and the introduction of community care policies and legislation has meant that it has played an increasing and significant role in the closure programmes of long-stay institutions. Schemes are often developed by housing associations and, to a lesser extent, local authorities in collaboration with social services and health agencies who are usually responsible for providing and financing the care and support. However, housing agencies have developed many schemes for people whose needs are not recognised in the community care legislation and are not given priority by social services or health agencies. Examples are schemes for ex-offenders or homeless young people. These are the schemes which are most threatened by any restriction on the scope of housing benefit.

The development of a supported accommodation project is often a difficult and protracted process with the need to enlist the active support of many agencies and to secure funding from a number of sources. Calls for a simple and adequate means of funding-supported housing have not been met and during the 1990s the resulting uncertainty has caused a reluctance by many housing agencies to be involved in what is increasingly perceived as a risky endeavour.

Conclusion

This chapter has set the context for the remainder of this book. It has outlined major social and economic policy and political trends that have effected change in, and will continue to exert an influence on, the provision of housing and social care. If key professionals within these two essential fields of social welfare are to participate in active partnership with those people who require their services, then their work must be grounded in knowledge of and response to the multiplicity of structural problems their clients may face. The subsequent chapters explore the potential of relevant research for the development of practice at the boundaries of social care and housing.

References

Anderson, I., Kemp, P. and Quiglars, D. (1993) *Single Homeless People: A Report for the Department of the Environment.* London: HMSO.

Arblaster, L. and Hawtin, M. (1994) *Health, Housing and Social Policy.* London: Socialist Medical Association.

Blanc, M. (1994) 'Housing exclusion and citizenship.' In European Network of Housing Research, *Housing – Social Integration and Exclusion.* Karelsrund Strand, Denmark.

Burns, A. (1997) 'Behind closed doors.' *Roof,* March/April, 16.

Burrows, R. (1997) *Contemporary Patterns of Residential Mobility in Relation to Social Housing in England.* York: Centre for Housing Policy.

Burrows, R. and Walentowicz, B. (1992) *Homes Cost Less than Homelessness.* London: Shelter.

Butler, A., Oldman, C. and Greve, J. (1983) *Sheltered Housing for the Elderly.* London: George Allen and Unwin.

Chaplin, R., Jones, M., Martin, S., Pryke, M., Royce, C., Saw, P., Whitehead, C. and Hong Yang, J. (1995) *Rents and Risks: Investing in Housing Associations.* York: Joseph Rowntree Foundation.

Charles, N. (1994) 'The housing needs of women and children escaping domestic violence.' *Journal of Social Policy 23,* 4, October, 465–487.

Clapham, D and Munro, M. (1990) 'Ambiguities and contradictions in the provision of sheltered housing for older people.' *Journal of Social Policy 19,* 27–45.

Coulter, J. (1996) 'Housing – cut, cut and cut again.' *Roof,* January/February.

Department of the Environment (1993) *English House Condition Survey.* London: HMSO.

Department of the Environment (1995) *Provision for Social Housing – Background Analysis.* London: Department of the Environment, HMSO.

Department of the Environment/Welsh Office(1995) *Our Future Homes: Opportunity, Choice, Responsibility.* Cmnd 2901, London: HMSO.

Fitzgeorge-Butler, A. and Williams, P. (1995) 'Quality and social housing: irreconcilable partners?' In Kirkpatrick, I. and Lucio M. (eds) *The Politics of Quality in the Public Sector.* London: Routledge.

Ford, J., Kempson, E. and England, J. (1996) *Into Work? The Impact of Housing Costs and the Benefit System on People's Decision to Work.* York: Joseph Rowntree Foundation.

Forrest, R. and Kennett, P. (1994) 'Exclusionary regimes in housing provision.' In European Network of Housing Research, *Housing – Social Integration and Exclusion.* Denmark: Karelsrund Strand.

Gabe, J. and Williams, P. (1993) 'Women, crowding and mental health.' In R. Burridge and S. Ormandy (eds) *Unhealthy Housing.* London: E & FN Spon.

Henderson, J. and Karn, V. (1987) *Race, Class and State Housing: Inequality and the Allocation of Public Housing in Britain.* Birmingham: CURS.

Hills, J. (1993) *The Future of Welfare.* York: Joseph Rowntree Foundation.

HMSO (1977) *Housing Policy: A Consultative Document.* Cmnd 6851, London: HMSO.

Holmans, A.E. (1996) *Housing Demand and Need in Wales 1991–2011.* York: Joseph Rowntree Foundation.

Holmans, A.E. (1995) *Housing Demand and Need in England 1991–2011.* York: Joseph Rowntree Foundation.

Kirkpatrick, I. and Lucio, M. (eds) (1995) *The Politics of Quality in the Public Sector.* London: Routledge.

Leather, P. and Morrison, T. (1997) *The State of UK Housing: A Factfile on Dwelling Conditions.* Bristol: The Policy Press.

Lee, P., Murie, A., Marsh, A. and Riseborough, M. (1995) *The Price of Social Exclusion.* London: National Federation of Housing Associations.

Lowry, J. (1991) *Housing and Health.* Plymouth: British Medical Journal.

Lund, B. (1996) *Housing Problems and Housing Policy.* London: Longman.

McClusky, J. (1997) *Where There's a Will...Developing Single Homelessness Strategies.* London: CHAR.

Malos, E. and Hague, G. (1993) *Domestic Violence and Housing: Local Authorities' Responses to Women Escaping Violent Homes?* Bristol Papers in Applied Social Studies, no. 19. Bristol: Women's Aid Federation England/School of Applied Social Studies, Bristol.

Midgley, G., Munlo, I. and Brown, M. (1997) *Sharing Power: Integrating User Involvement and Multi-Agency Working to Improve Housing for Older People.* Bristol: Policy Press.

National Federation of Housing Associations (1993) *Single Women in Housing Need: Improving Access to Housing Association Homes.* London: NFHA.

National Institute for Social Work (1996) 'Social exclusion, civil society and social work.' *Briefing 18.* ttp://www.nisw.org.uk/polb/fulltext/niswb18.html

Newton, J. (1994) *All in One Place: The British Housing Story 1973–1993.* London: Catholic Aid Housing Society.

Pfeffer, N. and Coote, A. (1991) *Is Quality Good for You? A Critical Review of Quality Assurance in Welfare Services.* London: Institute of Public Policy Research.

Rossi, P. (1987) 'No good applied social research goes unpunished.' *Society 25,* 73–79.

Shaw, I., Bloor, M. and Roberts, S. (1996) *Without Shelter: Estimating Rooflessness in Scotland.* Edinburgh: Central Research Unit, Scottish Office.

Shelter (1995) *Shelter's Response to the White Paper.* London: Shelter.

Smailes, J. (1994) 'Lesbians' experience of housing.' In R. Gilroy and R. Woods (eds) *Housing Women.* London: Routledge.

Smith, S. (1989) *The Politics of 'Race' and Residence.* London: Polity Press.

Stewart, G. and Stewart, J. (1992) *Social Work and Housing.* London: Macmillan.

Townsend, P. (1962) *The Last Refuge.* London: Routledge and Kegan Paul.

Watson, S. and Austerberry, H. (1986) *Housing and Homelessness: A Feminist Perspective.* London: Routledge.

CHAPTER 2

Practice and Research for Housing the Socially Excluded

Ian Shaw

The starting point for this book is the threefold weakness of social workers' hold on the significance of housing issues, manifested in the restriction of social work interest to issues of special needs and acute housing malaise, a lack of analytical backbone, and a recurrent tendency to declining engagement and withdrawal.

The decline and withdrawal of social work interest is not, of course, unanimous or complete. Some social workers retain a commitment to tackling homelessness, and to addressing the accommodation and shelter dimensions of those with mental health problems, young people leaving care, single homeless people with drug and alcohol problems, women at risk of domestic violence, people with learning disabilities, and those faced with admission to homes for elderly people. However, most of the explanatory frameworks and models of intervention which social workers favour do not have an obvious place for issues of housing. Theories of normalisation, applied especially in the special needs field to provision for people with learning disabilities and mental health problems, are one exception to this criticism, as are broader ideas of intervening in service users' social systems, but these are rare exceptions.

There are core parts of social work intervention where housing problems repeatedly tap the shoulders of social work practitioners. Community care is the field where housing issues have recently enjoyed the most prominence among social workers, and where the largest programme of research has taken place (reviewed by Watson 1997). Most of this work has been undertaken by people working from a housing perspective, and it is reasonable to assume that there is a considerable degree of ignorance among social workers, especially at the service delivery level, of the findings and conclusions of this research.

Work with offenders is another field where intervention by probation officers and social workers reflects housing issues. There was a well established line of Home Office supported, American-influenced research, dating from the 1960s, which emphasised the impact of social environments within which offenders live (e.g. Davies 1969, 1974). This took place alongside research on hostels and the borderline between home and institution, through the earlier research of Sinclair, Tizard and Clarke (e.g. Cornish and Clarke 1975; Sinclair 1970; Tizard, Sinclair and Clarke 1975). The years since the late 1970s have produced very little research which takes into account the housing and broader environmental contexts of probation practice (c.f. Drakeford and Vanstone 1996), although valuable research on the boundaries between home and institution has been carried out in the child care field through, for example, the Dartington Unit.

The flourishing of the housing association movement following the housing legislation of the mid 1970s, paradoxically, facilitated the distancing of social work and probation staff from special needs provision. The more recent establishment of National Standards for the Probation Service (e.g. Home Office 1995) has revived a focus on accommodation matters (through, for example, the establishment of Area Accommodation Forums, and new contractual arrangements with housing associations to provide and manage offender accommodation). Once more, however, this is limited by the inbuilt tendency of the Probation Service to farm out housing matters to external agencies, and by the withdrawal of probation officers from the management committees of housing associations in the mid 1990s. The best recent research in this field has been focused on the housing needs of young people. Jones' analysis of young people leaving home (Jones 1995) is an excellent example of research which locates housing and homelessness issues for young people in the broader context of housing markets and housing careers.

Some of the most innovative work on housing in the social work field has been carried out by the voluntary agencies, for example through collaborative projects between the major children's agencies and homelessness agencies in London and other large cities. The traditional principles upon which charitable agencies operate are that they are:

- non-profitable
- of public benefit

and that the

- trustees hold the role of altruistic custodians
- public and private agencies are independent
- voluntary bodies both *do* and contribute to the *debate about doing*.

Both the contract culture and the professionalisation of the voluntary sector challenge these principles, and have prompted fresh thinking regarding the role of the voluntary sector (e.g. Home Office 1990; Knight 1993). Behind these developments lie fundamental shifts in the relationship between charities and government, in which there has been a change from a full provider state to a mixed economy welfare state. The boundary between procuring and providing services lies at the heart of the question of the future of the voluntary sector (Shaw 1995). The central issue is the tension between being business-like and sustaining a concern for people's well-being.

These piecemeal and partial linkages between social care and housing are unlikely to be enriched through the training experiences of either social workers or housing managers. Housing training is almost always located separately from social work training programmes. Housing and social work academics are rarely based in the same departments or involved in joint teaching or research within higher education. There are frequently different social science enquiry traditions, and an absence of joint research. Social work placements in housing settings may, impressionistically, be slightly more common, although they are still a tiny minority of practice placements, and are concentrated in a small span of special needs settings. There has been a more general expectation that social work students will cover legislation regarding homelessness, but teaching on housing is often weak even in well-grounded social policy and sociology university departments. There has, however, been some valuable development work undertaken to make available a Level 4 NVQ award in Special Needs Housing which is recognised by both the Central Council for Education in Social Work and the Chartered Institute for Housing.

Social exclusion, housing and social care

The partial scope of social work interest and its lack of analytical backbone can be countered in part by an awareness of the knock-on effects of trends in home ownership and the wider housing market described in the previous chapter, but also by reconnecting social workers' grasp of the broader structural effects of political, economic, demographic and social contexts which constrain the housing opportunities of those with whom they work. We will argue, as does Stewart in the following chapter, that this lack of engagement can also be addressed through an analysis and response strategy based on social exclusion and inclusion.

There is persuasive evidence that the relationship between social care and housing will continue to be fragmented and lacking in purpose if it is divorced from wider structural explanations. These explanations will take on board the poverty of service users (Stewart), the inherent residualising and marginalising tendencies of youth policy (Drakeford and Williamson), the systemic disadvantaging of women (Wasoff) and the chronic direct and indirect racism of much housing and social work provision (Chakrabarti). They must also take into account and respond to the sharp criticisms of commentators who regard social work as at least as much the problem as it is the solution. For example, Carlen has voiced her concerns about the relationship between social and criminal justice. She holds the state responsible for what she regards as the failure of welfare and the increase of surveillance, punishment and anti-social control. Homelessness, in this view of things, is the product of social exclusion and 'failed liberal-democratic welfare states of the twentieth century' (Carlen 1996, p.11), marked by an 'asymmetrical citizenship' which allows the rich to escape punishment and cracks down with unremitting severity on the poor. She sees young people as part of a constituency of resistance to these punishing inequalities, in which they become survivors. Survivalism in a fractured world necessarily involves the reordering of political, moral and economic possibilities in such a way that young people are often criminogenic (p.82). Carlen is no friend of social workers. She attacks what she regards as agency-maintained homelessness, and a 'corrosive "dependency culture" spawned by an always and already inept welfarism' (p.43).

The reminder that social welfare can harm and exclude is salutary, though we are not persuaded by the quasi-revolutionary solutions implied by Carlen's analysis. Homeless people, petty criminals, New Age travellers, beggars on the streets, drug takers, lager louts, the unemployed, and dropouts in general have often been labelled the 'underclass'. The term 'has unusual power as a flexible buzzword...a synthesising notion which lumps together a disparate group of individuals' (Lee, Murie, Marsh and Riseborough 1995, p.36). Leaving aside popular images of the dangerous classes and American usage which too often serves to justify right wing politics and stigmatisation (c.f. Lister 1996), the essence of the underclass idea is of disconnection, usually for long periods of time, from the formal labour markets, and detachment from family life. Explanations for the development of an underclass may emphasise the behaviour of its members—they are poor because of the way they behave—or the impact of the economy on the lives of particular groups.

The mid1990s witnessed a sudden awakening among both politicians and professionals in the housing and welfare fields to the advocacy of social exclusion as an alternative analysis and policy basis. The National Housing Federation (formerly National Federation of Housing Associations) has been vocal in its call for a policy of social exclusion to attack the growing cancer of social polarisation, and the summer of 1997 was marked, at one end of the scale, by the first major British social work conference on social exclusion, and at the other end, by the launch of the Labour government's Social Exclusion Unit chaired by the Prime Minister. Indeed, social exclusion, until recently an unwelcome reminder to British politicians of the Maastricht Treaty's Social Chapter, is now in danger of becoming faddish.

Which line of analysis is likely to prove more powerful to those working in the social care and housing field? Forrest and Kennett have few doubts.

> While the concept of the underclass is problematic it nevertheless retains an emphasis on an interpretation of society as vertically stratified - unlike broader concepts (such as social exclusion) which convey the possibility for consensus in a horizontally differentiated society. (Forrest and Kennett 1994, p.140)

The question is largely one of policy responses rather than social explanation. We believe it is right to conclude that

> the term 'social exclusion' draws attention to the same issues embraced by 'underclass' and has the advantage of focusing on processes as well as avoiding the ideological loading so often attached to 'underclass'...It is deprivation and exclusion that should be the target for policy makers, rather

than the possible emergence of an underclass. To focus on the underclass is to be concerned with effects rather than causes. (Lee, Murie, Marsh and Riseborough 1995, p.39)

Social exclusion implies the need for a wider approach to debates about inequality than is often adopted. It links to ideas regarding active citizenship which we earlier identified with housing exclusion, and access to housing, health care, social work, employment and education. Attention is therefore directed towards the multifarious nature of the disadvantage which creates exclusion, its long-term persistence, the intractability of social exclusion to western welfare state solutions, and the concentration of disadvantage on certain groups. It enjoys common ground with several other ideas and policies, including ideals of a civil society mentioned previously in relation to central and eastern European countries, communitarian ideas associated with Amitai Etzioni and currently the subject of debate in America, and the Labour government's Welfare to Work policies. Social exclusion policies place greater emphasis on an active, 'stakeholder' role for citizens in the development of social policy, unlike the mixture of consumerism and market choice which characterised previous governments' promotion of the Citizens' Charter.

The consequences for social care and housing of adopting a policy of social exclusion are far reaching. They will lead to changes in social work practice, forms of service development and delivery, social work training, and the agenda for research.

The practice of social care

The seeds of the division of British social work from community development and community organisation lay in the establishment of integrated social work and social services departments from 1970 onwards. Separate training developed for community workers and social workers, and community work projects gradually withered from the mid1970s with the demise of the Home Office-sponsored Community Development Projects. We suggest below that policies designed to combat social exclusion will depend on collaborative and integrated community-based human services, then

Within this integrated approach the role of the social worker as community development worker will come more to the fore...The challenges of reducing social exclusion through working with those individuals and groups currently denied access to employment or services demands new approaches. These must incorporate both the understandings drawn from current social work practice and those from community development...(and) building a community infrastructure with emphasis on self help and participation. (National Institute for Social Work 1996)

Marcuse has commented on the walled and quartered cities of the United States, comprised of the gentrified quarter, the suburban city, the tenement city, and the abandoned city (e.g. Marcuse 1994). The abandoned city is where 'home-less housing' is most often found, and where socially palpable walls create spatial segregation and reinforce social hierarchies. Practising within an integrated social work and community development role, social workers are more likely to penetrate beyond their insufficient awareness of the spatial dimension of people's lives.

Partnership policies

If disadvantage has multiple causes then the implications are that

policies must be developed across the barriers between departments, sectors, levels of government and disciplines. It is essential that strategic approaches are adopted which involve a holistic, multi-disciplinary, cross-departmental and partnership approach. (Lee, Murie, Marsh and Riseborough 1995, p.45)

Social inclusion policies offer no easy panacea, and will require sustained responses based on both national, or even European, frameworks and local strategies. However, universal strategies must not assume a homogenous, European normality, and local diversity must not lead to a free-for-all atomisation and loss of solidarity. European social work must be intercultural, it must confront issues of social exclusion, and it must develop an intervention that deals with both personal and collective identities (Lorenz 1994).

The beginnings of a coherent assessment of practices and policies that will facilitate social inclusion have been attempted in a project on Social Work and Social Exclusion in Europe, co-ordinated by the International Federation of Social Workers and funded by the European Commission. The project reported in 1997 with the aim of demonstrating practical ways in which social workers across Europe

were promoting social inclusion, and recommending ways of developing policy at
EU, national and professional levels.

Training for social care and housing

Changed forms of practice and new patterns of partnership and service collaboration call for new attitudes to training for work in the field of housing and social
care. We highlighted the gaps between professional training for housing managers and social workers earlier in this chapter. We also regret the separation of training for social workers and practitioners in the community development field. We
are not in favour of merged training, but the absence of any joint training between
social workers and housing managers, and the limited degree to which shared
learning happens in the community development field, demand urgent and early
changes. Wiseman and Hayton (Chapter 6) detail necessary syllabus headings for
shared training.

Research agendas

Policies of social inclusion will promote a new research agenda, which asks new
questions and which is premised on new partnerships. A working party on homelessness was established by France's Conseil National de l'Information Statistique
(CNIS) and reported in 1996. CNIS provides a forum for producers and users of
public statistics and co-ordinates government statistical activities. The working
party's focus on explanations and policies based on social exclusion and inclusion
supported the following conclusions:

- Government departments must include measures of social exclusion~in
  official statistics.

- It is at the local level that the match between housing supply and demand can
  be appreciated, and data disaggregated to the local level must be produced.

- Research on homelessness ought to address 'fundamental questions of how
  and why rather than how many' (CNIS 1996). The working party drew up a
  list of situations of exclusion from housing, classified according to levels of
  precariousness.

- The population of the homeless only exists in the wider context of the total
  home-owning population. Reflecting on associated research carried out in

Paris by INED (Institut National d'Etude Démographiques) Marpsat and Firdion conclude that 'Preventive policy on homelessness must not just seek to keep people in their homes and give them access to housing, but contribute to the more general combat against all aspects of poverty' (Marpsat and Firdion 1996).

Research which aims to provide 'how many' estimates of the prevalence of homelessness is not as redundant as the CNIS report suggests (c.f. Shaw, Bloor, Cormack and Williamson 1996), but the positive point made by the authors is important. Policies and research which focus on social exclusion will pose questions such as how certain groups of people become homeless (the process of social exclusion), how they organise their own survival, how people leave homelessness, and who gets back into homelessness (inclusion and re-exclusion).

Social inclusion policies shape not only the agenda of questions for research enquiry, but also the way in which research is conducted. Extensions of ideas of empowerment have already created interest in models of partnership research and research as a form of emancipation. Social research which is premised on an assumption that people are likely to be excluded, has also led to research partnerships which include enhanced communication with the excluded. However, there is a central and perhaps inescapable paradox in social research. The need to know is based on the one hand on a wish to make a social problem visible and to empower people to combat that problem. Yet knowledge of a problem may lead to growth in social control, and efforts to make a problem visible may make people more likely to live for the record and to avoid visibility. The social worker and the researcher have to work with the paradox that they seek to be empowering and yet in so doing risk increasing people's marginality - the wish to understand in itself increases the risk of greater social exclusion.

A stronger collaborative research effort between social workers across Europe will also strengthen research which is relevant to both social work and housing. There is already a European Network of Housing Research (ENHR), and there is a strong case for developing a similar European Network for Social Work Research. Such a network would need to be established on a broad base, to have strong links with the ENHR, to work closely with officials from the European Commission, and to involve collaboration across the damaging divide between English-speaking and French-speaking social work.

Equal opportunities for social care and housing

Housing policies in the years following the establishment of the Welfare State were marked by inclusionary policy aims of housing as a social right, universal subsidies, tax breaks and direct state housing provision. There were, however, equal opportunity problems raised by this earlier housing regime. It elevated the white, male industrial worker as citizen and was built on the partial citizenship of women and members of ethnic minorities. In Forrest and Kennett's words, 'the boundaries of social rights are constructed within specific discourses which legitimate the exclusion of, for example, women and ethnic minorities from full citizen status and which reinforces boundaries between the deserving and the undeserving' (Forrest and Kennett 1994 p.131). Economic and political shifts from the mid1970s pushed housing policies in a more exclusionary direction, with the hardening of 'tenure closure' whereby minorities are unable to compete in the housing market. The lower the status hierarchy of housing the greater the proportion of ethnic minority and women headed households.

Research into housing aspects of community care and care and support, discussed later in this chapter, has not typically placed strong emphasis on issues of race or gender, and this is one area where social work practice and thinking has been stronger than for work done in the housing field. Of the research reviewed by Watson, only one study specifically focused on issues of race (Radia 1996; c.f. Watson 1997). In her study of the housing needs of Asian people with mental health problems in two London boroughs, Radia concludes that the services which were available were not culturally sensitive and did not cater for those who were not fluent in spoken or written English. The double disadvantage of being an Asian and having a mental health problem placed many people in a situation where they were unlikely to use the services. A welcome initiative in this area is the paper from the Commission for Racial equality, the Chartered Institute of Housing and the Association of Directors of Social Services, which identifies an agenda for action in addressing issues of race and culture in the field of community care (Commission for Racial Equality 1997).

An underlying problem, also explored by Chakrabarti in this book, is that professionals and policy makers continue to operate on the basis of untested assumptions about how Asian people live and think. The assumptions that mental health problems are the same in every culture, that no one is asking for a service so there is no need for it, and that language problems do not exist for people who have lived in Britain for some time, all tighten the screws of double jeopardy faced by Asian service users.

Practitioners in the social care and housing field are bound by the Race Relations Act 1976, as amended by the Housing Act 1988, the Sex Discrimination Act 1975, as amended in 1986, the Equal Pay Act 1970 (amended 1984), the Disabled Persons Employment Act 1944 (amended 1958), and by European legislation and directives in the field of sex equality. Within these legal contexts the Commission for Racial Equality (CRE), the Housing Corporation and the National Housing Federation (NHF) expect housing agencies to set targets, although the CRE and the NHF are both at pains to distinguish between targets (permitted) and quotas (not permitted, with the partial exception of employment quotas for people with a disability). The NHF has produced a draft code of practice for tackling discrimination and promoting racial equality (National Housing Federation 1997) and may develop similar codes for other equal opportunity issues in the future. The International Federation of Social Workers has argued for a European treaty on social rights, which should be subject to judicial review, and would include rights

- to family life and relationships of choice
- to be integrated or not according to personal choice
- to housing
- to education
- to health care
- of children and young people to be treated as citizens.

This proposal reflects similar arguments put forward by leaders in the field of supported housing and is a further area where social work and housing collaboration would advantage service users in the field of supported housing (Palmer 1995).

Developing good practice

We have illustrated ways in which conceptual and analytical reflection, rooted mainly in the disciplines of sociology and social policy, gives purpose and 'bite' to thinking about social care and housing. Several of the writers in this book demonstrate ways in which such an approach can be developed. Other contributors start more directly with practice questions, eliciting the lessons for good housing and social care practice which follow from recent research. There are several general consequences which can be drawn from these contributions to the book. The largest field in which practice-oriented research has been carried out is community care, and this is where Oldman, Allen, Wiseman and Hayton, and Franklin concentrate their attention. This research has focused largely on four linked domains, *viz*, the difficulties of accomplishing effective shared planning decisions, tensions between the relative roles of social workers and housing managers in needs assessment, initiatives in the field of special needs care and support, and developments in intervention models. Each of these practice domains has yielded some degree of formalised effort to codify practice, and several useful codes have been published during the 1990s, largely initiated by writers commencing from a housing perspective (e.g. Clapham and Franklin 1994; Watson and Conway 1995). The Nolan Committee on public standards reported directly on housing associations, in connection with which the National Federation of Housing Associations (National Housing Federation) produced a widely acclaimed code of governance.

Community care planning and assessment

Boundary disputes between social workers and housing officers are often heated. Housing staff feel that social workers are leaving them to fill the gaps. Social workers feel that housing officers unrealistically expect them to pick up every problem, and that a more socially oriented role should be part of the housing managers' task. In 1995 the Chartered Institute of Housing (CIH) produced a good practice guide on the development of local strategies for housing and community care. Although government guidance had previously promoted collaboration between housing, social services and health authorities, it had been sparse and in the view of some commentators reflected the tensions between the Department of Health and the Department of the Environment. In addition, each sector traditionally approaches strategic thinking in a different way. In housing, thinking is oriented primarily around properties and different tenures. In social services, thinking often centres on different service user groups, while in the health field the location and type of service (e.g. primary care) frequently provides the focus. The good practice strategy in the CIH guide covers both the infrastructure of accommodation and support, and the mechanisms by which people gain access to housing and support. It includes ten policy objectives which can be used to inform the appraisal of existing provision and the development of service proposals. The recommendation is for a coherent network of provision which offers a degree of choice between different kinds of accommodation and support. The forms of provision that experience suggests will be underdeveloped include small schemes of grouped self-contained flats, networks of dispersed flats linked to a resettlement team, houses and flats designed to 'Lifetime Homes' standards, small shared houses with good individual facilities, staffed emergency/crisis accommodation, and extra care sheltered accommodation.

Collaboration has been the subject of sound good practice guidance. Stewart observes in the following chapter that it has come to occupy a status as one of the holy grails of modern social policy. Despite this, collaboration between housing, health and social services agencies is difficult to achieve. Allen develops a critical analysis of the joint working agenda in Chapter Five. Recent research suggests seven areas where barriers to effective collaboration exist (Arblaster, Conway, Foreman and Hawtin 1996).

- There is little evidence of three-way links between all the agencies. Links between social services and health are reasonably good, but both tend to exclude housing.

- The introduction of markets into the provision of social care has tended to militate against collaborative working, through the stimulation of a competitive climate.

- There remains widespread misunderstanding about the roles and responsibilities of other agencies, especially between the voluntary and statutory sectors.

- There are serious shortfalls in provision for people with medium and low levels of need who are not given priority in community care provisions.

- Collaboration may exist at strategic levels but this is often not reflected in the delivery of services.

- User involvement is restricted to choice between a limited range of existing options rather than the development of wider choices. In addition such involvement is usually at the individual level and very rarely at the level of strategic planning.

- Finally, there is no clear national level mechanism or agenda within which
  local agencies operate.

Research has helpfully identified the problems, but authors of future enquiry need
to address the evaluation of new forms of collaboration. A valuable example of
such work is provided by Lund and Foord (1997), who analysed 120 housing
strategies produced each year between 1993 and 1995, and also reviewed the
community care plans associated with these strategies. They conclude that housing authorities' role in community care planning has been enhanced, although
there continues to be a lack of 'bottom up' information to aggregate need and formulate ways of estimating the national requirement for accommodation arising
from community care. In addition Lund and Foord observe that there tends to be
an assumption that particular need is absent simply because it has not been quanti-
fied.

Housing authorities are responding to their disquiet regarding the unmet support needs of their tenants by establishing support teams and by linking offers of
accommodation to guarantees of care/support packages from social services and
the voluntary sector. There continue to be problems regarding the spatial concentration of special needs housing and the available powers to promote 'balanced
communities' are rarely used. Lund and Foord observe that in the 1990s the debate
on housing and community care has focused on the process of joint working rather
than the outcomes of collaboration, but believe that there are now sufficient examples of good practice to justify the establishment of a new centre to collect and dis-
seminate information.

Arblaster and colleagues concluded that collaboration may exist at strategic levels but this is not often reflected in the delivery of services (Arblaster, Conway,
Foreman and Hawtin 1996). The different perspectives of staff in social work,
housing and health may easily lead to conflict over need assessment. There is a
duty to consult over need assessment but it appears that

> in most cases...assessments are being carried out by staff of social services
> departments with housing only being contacted if there is considered to be an
> important housing dimension. (Clapham and Franklin 1994, p.12)

There are obvious problems with this practice. It leaves social workers with the
task of deciding what counts as a housing problem, and, paradoxically, it under-

mines the case that social workers often wish to make that housing managers should have a social role. Clapham and Franklin have listed the main arguments presented for and against housing staff carrying a social role (1994, pp.18-19), and it is reasonable to conclude that social workers are not always sufficiently aware of the countervailing pressures under which housing staff operate.

Social care practice

Arblaster and colleagues argue that user involvement is restricted to choice between a limited range of existing options rather than the development of wider choices. In addition such involvement is usually at the individual level and very rarely at the level of strategic planning. It is our view that research regarding user involvement should be carried out in ways which themselves enhance participation. In their research on problems of assessment, information provision and planning in the housing system for older people Midgley, Munlo and Brown (1997) undertook the design of improvements through workshops with older people in receipt of housing services, carers and representatives from community groups and voluntary organisations, and managers and front line professionals. They produced a persuasive account of what the best possible practice would look like, and were able to identify an innovative model of integrated multi-agency working and user involvement which should be able to deliver this best practice. Of particular relevance to the arguments made here and later in this book, they insist that, although their model was developed with housing services for older people in mind, the model may be adapted and applied to any multi-agency service system.

The studies by Lund and Foord, and by Midgley, Munlo and Brown exemplify the direction in which research on social care and housing needs to move. There are, however, serious problems which such research and consequent practice will need to address. In a discussion of the findings from twenty one research studies in housing and community care carried out between 1993 and 1996 Watson (1997) identifies two key themes which thread through all the studies. These are the integration of housing and support within mainstream provision, and the influence of the service user in the design and delivery of services. These recurring themes affect where people live, the reality of choice, the assessment of needs, access to information and advice, and finding and funding support.

There are other practice issues, some of which are touched on in this book, but others of which remain largely marginal to research and practice. Development of good practice models in relation to social work and housing has been heavily dependent on research in community care. The implications of recent research on *women* in the housing market (for which Wasoff provides a valuable synthesis in this book) and practice development which follows from research in the area of work with *young people* (addressed here by Drakeford and Williamson, and by Stewart), are examples of enquiry and practice which have both remained too marginal to the development of social care and housing. There has been high quality research on social work with *children and families*, carried out, for example, through the Dartington Research Unit, but it has yet to be applied to the boundaries with housing.

Some of the available good practice guidance is wide enough to apply to *offenders*. The report following the death of Jonathan Newby, a volunteer worker killed by a resident at a registered care home managed by a voluntary agency and owned by a housing association, has led to work on organisational standards. New developments on NVQ *training*, and an interesting collaborative project between Stonham Housing Association—a leading special needs provider—and the National Institute for Social Work promise helpful outcomes on good practice. Very little attention has been given to the essential character of practice intervention in supported housing projects. Is it a species of residential social work—that is, social work but carried out in a special *setting*—or is there a form of practice, *project work* for want of a more fitting label, which is distinctive to initiatives and schemes of this kind? Social workers have been educated to insist that social work is a generic core of practice which is applied to a variety of settings. There have been sound reasons for pursuing this line of argument, linked to efforts to improve standards of practice in residential establishments, but it risks militating against flexibility in developing appropriate models of intervention in the field of social care and housing.

Social workers should also be at the centre of developing alternative ways of linking housing and support. Despite the problems which have been associated with its implementation, the development of *'floating support'* schemes (Morris 1995) and debate about the value of a voucher system and direct payments to promote a more flexible person-centred rather than property-based allowance (Clapham, Munroe and Kay 1994) are among the more imaginative ideas and practices to arrive on the scene during the 1990s, whereby people should not need to move *accommodation* in order to gain *support*.

Finally, the implications of developments in *technology* have been too little appreciated thus far. New technologies have been neglected in both housing and social work research. There is also little awareness of the direct practice implications and potential of new technology. For example, there is a very active electronic discussion list (*Homeless*) used heavily in the United States by homeless people as well as staff of homelessness agencies, which provides a forum of debate and an electronic community, neither of which exist in Britain.

Conclusion

We have outlined the problems and progress of practice and research at the boundaries of social care and housing, and have argued that an understanding based on social exclusion will exercise an important shaping influence on the practice of social care. It will provide a strong rationale for partnership between agencies, and has practical implications for professional training in both social work and housing. An agenda of understanding and countering social exclusion will also stimulate and give an overall coherence to research on social care, housing and homelessness.

Social exclusion does not, however, provide an exhaustive basis for social care and housing. We have also explored the ways in which good practice can be developed on the back of recent research in this field. Such concerns—of analysis and of good practice—underlie the following chapters.

References

Arblaster, L., Conway, J., Foreman, A. and Hawtin, M. (1996) *Setting Us Up to Fail? A Study of Inter-agency Working to Address Housing, Health and Social Care Needs of People in General Needs Housing.* York: Joseph Rowntree Foundation.

Carlen, P. (1996) *Jigsaw: A Political Criminology of Youth Homelessness.* Buckingham: Open University Press.

Clapham, D. and Franklin, B. (1994) *Housing Management, Community Care and Competitive Tendering: A Good Practice Guide.* London: Chartered Institute of Housing.

Clapham, D., Munroe, M. and Kay, H. (1994) *A Wider Choice: Revenue Funding Mechanisms for Housing and Community Care.* York: Joseph Rowntree Foundation.

Commission for Racial Equality (1997) *Race, Culture and Community Care: The Agenda for Action.* London: CRE.

Conseil National de L'Information Statistique (1996) 'Towards a better understanding of the homeless and exclusion from housing.' *Actualities 17,* May.

Cornish, D. and Clarke, R. (1975) *Residential Treatment and its Effects on Delinquency.* London: HMSO.

Davies, M. (1969) *Probationers in Their Social Environment.* London: HMSO.

Davies, M. (1974) *Social Work in the Environment.* London: HMSO.

Forrest, R. and Kennett, P. (1994) 'Exclusionary regimes in housing provision.' In European Network of Housing Research, *Housing – Social Integration and Exclusion,* Karelsrund Strand, Denmark.

Home Office (1990) *Efficiency Scrutiny of Government Funding of the Voluntary Sector.* London: HMSO.

Home Office (1995) *National Standards for the Supervision of Offenders in the Community.* London: Home Office.

Jones, G. (1995) *Leaving Home.* Buckingham: Open University Press.

Knight, B. (1993) *Voluntary Action.* London: CENTRIS.

Lee, P., Murie, A., Marsh, A. and Riseborough, M. (1995) *The Price of Social Exclusion.* London: National Federation of Housing Associations.

Lister, R. (ed) (1996) *Charles Murray and the Underclass: The Developing Debate.* London: Institute of Economic Affairs.

Lorenz, W. (1994) *Social Work in a Changing Europe.* London: Routledge.

Lund, B. and Foord, M. (1997) *Toward Integrated Living: Housing Strategies and Community Care.* Bristol: The Policy Press.

Marcuse, P. (1994) 'The walled and quartered cities of the United States: convergent trends with European cities?' In European Network of Housing Research, *Housing – Social Integration and Exclusion,* Karelsrund Strand, Denmark.

Marpsat, M. and Firdion, J-M. (1996) 'Becoming homeless: who is at risk?' *Population et Sociétés* (Bulletin of Institut National d'Etudes Démographiques), May.

Midgley, G., Munlo, I. and Brown, M.(1997) *Sharing Power: Integrating User Involvement and Multi-Agency Working to Improve Housing for Older People.* Bristol: Policy Press.

Morris, J. (1995) *Housing and Floating Support.* York: Joseph Rowntree Foundation.

National Housing Federation (1997) *Draft Code of Practice for Tackling Discrimination and Promoting Racial Equality.* London: National Housing Federation.

National Institute for Social Work (1996) 'Social exclusion, civil society and social work.' *Briefing 18.* ttp://www.nisw.org.uk/polb/fulltext/niswb18.html

Palmer, J. (1995) 'Social disadvantage and social exclusion: the need for a definition of rights.' Unpublished paper to Congress of International Federation for Housing and Planning, Belfast.

Radia, K. (1996) *Ignored, Silenced Neglected: Housing and Mental Health Care Needs of Asian People.* York: Joseph Rowntree Foundation.

Shaw, I. (1995) 'The quality of mercy: the management of quality in the personal social services.' In I. Kirkpatrick and M. Lucio (eds) *The Politics of Quality in the Public Sector.* London: Routledge.

Shaw, I., Bloor, M., Cormack, R. and Williamson, H. (1996) 'Estimating the prevalence of hard-to-reach populations: the illustration of mark-recapture methods in the study of homelessness.' *Social Policy and Administration 30,* 1, 69–85.

Sinclair, I. (1970) *Hostels for Probationers.* London: HMSO.

Tizard, J., Sinclair, I. and Clarke, R. (eds) (1975) *Varieties of Residential Experience.* London: Routledge.

Watson, L. (1997) *High Hopes: Making Housing and Community Care Work.* York: Joseph Rowntree Foundation.

Watson, L. and Conway, T. (1995) *Homes for Independent Living: Housing and Community Care Strategies.* Coventry: Chartered Institute of Housing.

CHAPTER 3

Housing, Poverty and Social Exclusion

Gill Stewart

Poverty and housing problems are inextricably linked to the profile of social work agency caseloads throughout the country and to the experience of most service users. These links were exemplified in Tony Blair's choice of the vast 'difficult to let' Aylesbury council estate in Southwark as the place from which to make his first prime ministerial speech on welfare (reported in *The Guardian,* 3 June 1997, p.1). The policies which he trailed then–reintegrating benefit claimants into a culture of paid employment, unifying public services to support cohesive communities–reflected the themes of social exclusion and inclusion which have been central to academic and poverty lobby debates in the 1990s (Driver and Martell 1997). Two months later the New Labour government announced plans for a Social Exclusion Unit to co-ordinate social policies across the range of central government activity. The concept had entered the policy arena.

In this chapter I look at objective and subjective meanings of social exclusion, particularly in relation to housing, and their relevance to social work. Focusing on accounts of homelessness, I consider what makes the lived experience of exclusion and marginalisation something qualitatively different from the demographic fact of housing inequality, and how both social work and housing services may become part of the excluding process. Finally I suggest how structural disadvantage and social exclusion can be challenged, both collaboratively and separately, through anti-oppressive practice in social work and housing services.

Theory

Theories of 'social exclusion' and the allied concept of 'underclass' were taken up by certain academics and poverty lobbyists, at the turn of the 1980s–1990s, as a way of moving beyond a rather tired old debate about definitions of relative versus absolute poverty and the search for ultimate methods of measurement (Dean 1992; Becker 1997; Lister 1990; Smith 1992). Some commentators (e.g. Jordan 1996) have presented social exclusion in economic and structural terms, as: the long-term exclusion of socially powerless groups from legitimate economic activity in the labour market, and the consequent production of an underclass dependent on state benefits, who are below the conventional social class stratification which is based on occupation. Others (e.g. Golding 1986) have presented social exclusion in cultural terms, as: the exclusion of 'the poor' from participation in culturally normative activities, such as celebrating Christmas, because they cannot afford it; and exclusion of the minority who must rent from participation in the 'property owning democracy'.

Another cultural account sees the 'underclass' as self-excluding, through their own behaviour, from the advantages and responsibilities of a capitalist society, preferring to be maintained at public expense in a 'culture of dependency'. Both the contemporary American and historical British versions of this account are essentially based on moral judgements, labelling and apportioning blame. A distinction is drawn between the 'deserving' and 'undeserving' poor with an argument that the latter's circumstances are due to choice or inadequacy and they must be disciplined and deterred for the general good (Lister 1996; Mann 1992; Morris 1994). Social policies which have been derived from these concepts seek to exclude 'undeserving' groups from access to state benefits and services. Challenging both the legality and morality of such a policy approach an appeal court judge said, when giving his ruling on the case of four London councils' treatment of homeless asylum seekers: 'I see no good reason why someone likely to suffer "injury or detriment" through a total inability to clothe, feed or shelter himself should be any less entitled to priority housing than someone vulnerable through age or disablement' (Lord Justice Brown reported in *The Guardian* 26 June 1996, p.4).

The underclass concept has been adopted by both sides of the party political spectrum in 1990s Britain but with some ambivalence, each suspecting that its use could imply some negative association with the other. Thus the director of the

Centre for Policy Studies, a New Right 'think tank', warned that, 'The term "underclass" is highly charged politically...it could well be a quasi-Marxist concept'. So he recommended that it should be used 'provisionally and hypothetically, and enclosed within imaginary quotation marks' (Willetts in Smith 1992, p.49). Similarly many on the political Left have understood 'underclass' as being part of a victim-blaming rightist agenda for pathologising poverty (Smith 1992, pp.3-4). Nevertheless two maverick Labour politicians aligned themselves with the concept, one of them a future Social Security Minister (Dennis 1997; Field 1989), and prominent 'critical' academics have been prepared to debate it under the auspices of the right-wing Institute of Economic Affairs (e.g. in Lister 1996). It is conceded that despite its 'disreputable pedigree' the underclass concept 'may have some value in progressive political discourse' (Robinson and Gregson 1992).

The integration of theorising about social exclusion into contemporary academic and political thinking marks a shift in emphasis within the poverty debate, from the measurement and adjustment of economic inequality to broader concerns about injustice and social cohesion. Social exclusion has therefore become an issue for anti-discriminatory and anti-oppressive practice in social work. Applying Thompson's (1997) analytical model we need to consider how the concept operates, in relation to housing, at structural, cultural and personal levels and what can be learned from this for social work practice.

Policy structure

The main structural divisions in British housing are: first, between the 70 per cent of the population who own their homes and the 30 per cent who rent or have no home; and second, between people who pay privately for their housing from earned income or other means, and those who have to rely on state benefits. Tenants, people who are homeless and benefit claimants are subject to regulation under social security and housing policies in ways which privately financed owner-occupiers are not.

The social policies of the Thatcher years, and since, have been characterised as 'anti-social policy' because of their ideologically derived intention to control and discipline through 'punitive and coercive forms of social policy frequently deployed under the mantle of "welfare"' (Squires 1990). Perhaps the clearest example of this was a series of measures, from the mid-1980s, which targeted unemployed single young people who were not living with a parent. First they were subject to special rules which forced them to move on from B & B (bed and breakfast) hostels to another area after a short period or take a drastic cut in benefit; then the abolition of Board and Lodging Regulations effectively closed the B & B option altogether (Chapman and Cook 1988). Under 21 year olds with jobs were removed from the protection of Wages Councils, on the argument that they were pricing themselves out of work by demanding high wages.

Age-related income support was introduced with a lower rate for under 25 year olds because, it was argued by ministers, they were not really independent and should have been living with their parents. But the parents of those young people who did stay at home had their housing benefit reduced by a 'non-dependent deduction', to offset rent which they were supposed to get from their children. Then under-18s were disqualified altogether from claiming benefit in their own right, unless they could prove estrangement from parents and that they would otherwise suffer 'severe hardship'. Most recently 'young individuals', single and under-25, are subject to a local restriction in housing benefit which is set at the level of rent for a bedsit, thereby forcing them into flatshares and hostels.

The explicit intention of these measures is to make young people live with a parent, or in nothing better than shared accommodation,[1] until they can finance their own independence with earnings from low-paid employment. Provisions to protect those without parents or who have been in care are discretionary and effectively require the advocacy of a social worker, thereby implicating social workers in the operation of a repressive set of policies which exclude young people from the resources required to sustain even a basic standard of independent living.

Another 'anti-social' policy with a discriminatory impact on users of social work services seems to be a case of policy conflict rather than the deliberate exclusion of an 'undeserving' group, more indifference and confusion than conspiracy. Changes to housing benefit during the 1980s made the 'care costs' in supported accommodation, such as adult placement schemes, 'ineligible' for refund through the benefits system, along with the rent, unless they were registered as residential care homes. There were three main problems with this: conditions of registration

---

1   This has been a necessarily simplified account of complex benefit regulations; anyone faced with a
     real situation should seek advice or consult a rights guide.

made informal types of supported accommodation institutionalised, with safety regulations and fire escapes; the procedures were complicated and expensive, deterring small providers; residents became disqualified from receiving a range of benefits to which they would otherwise be entitled. All of this goes against the objectives of normalisation and independent living which are central to community care policy.

The inherent conflict which is evident here between social security benefits policy and social services policy for community care has been pointed out frequently and recently (e.g. by Fimister 1995 and Griffiths 1996). However, central government appears disinclined to act, although they have done so previously when benefits payments were shown to be offering a 'perverse incentive' for older people to go into residential care, where the fees would be paid, instead of remaining in their own homes (Audit Commission 1986). Then the financial stakes for the treasury were high, whereas now there seems to be a lack of political and bureaucratic will to tackle a problem affecting only relatively small numbers of disabled social work service users, whose interests are easily marginalised by national policy makers.

Service users' housing: cultural contexts

The great majority of social work service users nationally live in social housing which is rented mainly from local authorities; similarly, up to 90 per cent of service users claim means tested benefits. Although data on housing tenure and benefits are not routinely collected everywhere, there is ample survey evidence and information from local studies for us to reach that conclusion (e.g. Bebbington and Miles 1989, and a wide range of sources are reviewed by Stewart and Stewart 1993a, Chapters 1 and 5). According to the data from such studies, service users in general fit the structural definition of social exclusion, being outside both the labour market and the dominant owner-occupied housing sector.

Looking more closely at where service users live, it is evident that they tend to come from the poorest areas, those wards which are identified by the national census as being most disadvantaged. These include particularly the mass housing estates which local authority landlords regard as 'difficult to let', and tenants experience as difficult to live in. As public sector housing became increasingly residualised during the 1980s, under pressure from the Thatcher government's 'right to buy' policy and squeeze on maintenance spending, more and more of the poorest families ended up living on those estates, often having previously been homeless (Burrows 1997a).

'Difficult' or, more perjoratively, 'problem' estates can be seen as the modern British equivalent of American 'ghettos' which were originally associated with cultural theories of poverty (Mann 1992; Morris 1994). New Right theorists (e.g. Murray in Lister 1996; Willetts in Smith 1992) point to a concentration of black lone mothers on benefits living on such estates, with high crime rates and child care problems generating heavy use of social work services, alleging that this constitutes a self-generating welfare-dependent underclass. However, Morris (1994) shows that evidence has been distorted and data manipulated to support the construction of a stereotype, when other interpretations would lead to different conclusions about the cultural contexts of poverty. Recent empirical research has tested those various interpretations and demonstrated that, in their own self-estimation, people who live in undesirable council housing estates on benefits and use social services do not necessarily become separated off from the rest of society. People defined as 'poor' generally see themselves neither as socially excluded passive victims of structural forces nor as self-excluding abusers of the welfare system. Rather they tend to share a range of more-or-less conventional, but seemingly unattainable, aspirations including a good job and their own home (Dean and Taylor-Gooby 1992; Jordan 1992; Shaw *et al.* 1996).

However, the distance between the supposed ideal and the reality of people's actual circumstances can promote feelings of second class citizenship, reflecting powerless anger at a welfare system which delays and obstructs legitimate claims and defensive pride at being able to sustain a basic standard of living despite the system (Dean and Melrose 1996). Bea Campbell's (1993) analysis of the riots which exploded on 'problem' housing estates around the country in the early 1990s records the despair and nihilism among young men which had resulted from economic and cultural exclusion without the hope of change. I have discussed elsewhere the difficulties reported by social workers and probation officers in relating to these alienated communities (Stewart and Stewart 1993a, Chapter 5). The powerlessness and insecurity which come from extreme inequality undermine social cohesion (Marris 1996; Wilkinson 1996).

Being homeless: personal meanings

While the conditions of life on mass housing estates illustrate issues in cultural explanations of social exclusion, the sharpest focus on their meanings at a personal level can be found in the experiences of people who have been homeless. It is 20 years since a government policy document first described homelessness as 'the most acute form of housing need' (DoE 1977) and the first specific primary legislation was passed. During that time the number of households officially recorded as 'statutorily' homeless almost trebled[2], with many others going unrecorded. In 1996 the Tory government repealed homeless people's right to priority rehousing (later to be restored by New Labour) on the grounds that it had given them an unfair advantage over those on council waiting lists.

Homelessness raises strong reactions (if inadequate action) from politicians and policy commentators; its increase has been described as epitomising the 'end of the modernist project', a reflection of failure in housing policy and an indictment of a civilised society (Daly 1996; Burrows 1997b). People with nowhere to live or only temporary accommodation are excluded, by lack of economic power, from opportunity in the housing market which is structured around ownership of property. They are excluded from 'social' housing by discriminatory policies and procedures which set priorities and deny access to certain groups, or offer them only the worst housing available. They are culturally excluded from participation in a home-based social life and from use of facilities which are dependent upon having an address (opening a bank account, obtaining credit, joining the public library, being on the electoral register).

My research on what social workers do in practice with homeless service users found it to be a mixture of advocacy, in negotiations with the benefits and housing systems, and support both for people who have been rejected by those systems and for those who are going through the official homelessness process, living indefinitely in hostels and other forms of temporary accommodation (Stewart and Stewart 1992). In order to provide effective advocacy and support, social workers need to understand the subjective meanings which people attach to their circum-

2   The source for this calculation is the homelessness statistics which were issued by the Department of the Environment half yearly then quarterly from 1978-1996.

stances; what being homeless signifies at a personal level. We are enabled to do this by the findings of qualitative research which chronicle the experiences of homeless people in a range of different settings.

Most of the regular women users of a day centre for homeless people in Brighton had become homeless, with and without children, in order to escape abuse from partners or family members or because they had been moved on by social services from children's homes or B & B accommodation which had been arranged for them as adults. To them 'home' meant safety and security, which had been lacking in their lives previously. 'Home' was also a base for personal identity and housing ceased to be home when safety and autonomy were threatened. Becoming homeless was seen as preferable to the housing options which were on offer - in mixed hostels, in short term sexual relationships with men - where they felt at risk and insecure. The researchers concluded that the housing available to these women had been the problem and that homelessness presented itself as a solution; the reverse of how the situation is usually construed by policy analysts (Tomas and Dittmar 1995).

There is by now a substantial body of research, much of it government funded, which considers the views and experiences of homeless single people, mostly men. Surveys of hostel residents show a common background of institutional living in children's homes, custody and mental hospitals. However most had left their last settled accommodation because of relationship breakdowns or family disputes, sometimes having been the perpetrators of domestic violence, or because they no longer felt safe when the resident population of a hostel changed. People who had to leave a hostel where they had settled, when it closed, often moved on again soon from the alternative placement because it was felt to be less satisfactory. A hostel cubicle can become a person's home, where they feel safe, however inadequate it is by housing criteria (Garside, Grimshaw and Ward 1990; Vincent, Deacon and Walker 1995). A report on homeless mental health service users described

> the alienation and mistrust, the isolation and the anger which were expressed in the interviews...Stigma is a major issue for people suffering from mental health problems. If, in addition, an individual also suffers the degradation of being homeless, the resulting erosion of self-esteem and sense of alienation from society is understandable, particularly since the majority of single homeless people with a mental health or substance misuse problem have

experienced a relationship breakdown, or bereavement, or have previously used the residential child care system and have little or no family support. Gaining access to services may be particularly difficult for homeless people as their voices are all too easily ignored. (Williams and Avebury 1995, p.37)

With even specialist open-access health services remaining underused by most rough sleepers, there has been a tendency to blame homeless people for their low use of health care. One recent report asked 'Are homeless people the underclass of the NHS?' (Fisher and Collins 1993). However, a qualitative study of homeless men's attitudes in East London found that there was considerable justification for the rough sleeping culture's tendency to undervalue mainstream health services, and concluded that 'they will use health services if they feel these are provided in an accessible and sensitive way' (Shiner 1995). If rough sleepers seem to be beyond the reach of the statutory and voluntary social services, the reason could be that health professionals and social workers make insufficient effort to offer their services appropriately (O'Leary 1997).

Research into the experience of homeless young people repeatedly shows what is now a familiar pattern: their reasons for becoming homeless are a combination of family conflict and being put out of social services accommodation, or institutions, with inappropriate offers of alternative housing (Biehal *et al.* 1995; Carlen 1996; Kirby 1994). Because of social policies which reduce young people's benefits, or disqualify them altogether (as discussed above), life without a job or family support can mean extreme poverty. So homeless young people easily become involved in survival offending—begging or stealing for food, prostitution—which carries the risk of criminalisation. This way of living can also be dangerous and there are high levels of victimisation among homeless young people. The fact that crimes committed against them are rarely pursued by the police, and therefore go unpunished, while the young people themselves (being 'of no fixed address') are dealt with harshly by the criminal justice system, tends to reinforce a sense of injustice and the feeling of exclusion from society (Carlen 1996; Ingram, Corning and Schmidt 1996; Stewart *et al.* 1994).

The danger and deprivation are real but they are only part of the mixed experiences reported by homeless young people, which also have a positive side. Homeless people in similar circumstances often show solidarity with each other and offer protection to members of their community who need it (Downing-Orr 1996).

Moreover, this protection may be extended to professionals working with them as I found in my own past experience as an outreach youth worker in central London. Living on the streets requires resilience and initiative and it often seems to be the most enterprising young people who take control of their lives by leaving intolerable situations and risking themselves in a strange city. For others it is a lifestyle choice to be 'on the move', rejecting convention and materialism despite the hardship (Jordan 1996, p.108).

It has been argued (most recently by Hutson and Liddiard 1994 and Carlen 1994) that homelessness in general, and 'youth homelessness' in particular, are socially constructed by the mainly voluntary agencies which set eligibility criteria and campaign for resources to 'help' homeless people by maintaining them in a circuit of substandard accommodation and segregated services. Insofar as there is truth in this argument, it implicates housing and social workers in the structural exclusion of a particularly vulnerable group of service users, and that is a serious matter.

Counteracting social exclusion

We need to consider how social work can respond to counteract social exclusion among service users at structural, cultural and personal levels and to facilitate their 'reconnection to the community' (Brown and Ziefert 1990). Challenging cultural stereotypes is a basic starting point, by avoiding disempowering language - 'vagrant', 'problem family', even 'underclass' and 'the poor' (Dean 1992) - and never colluding with negative assumptions about the character of people who are homeless or who live on notorious housing estates. At the personal level it is most important to listen to people's own interpretation of their circumstances, drawing out the positive strengths, which will be apparent in how they cope with stress and extreme hardship, and not just the problems.

It is essential for practitioners, under pressure from lack of resources and with few available solutions, to hold on to the principle that users are entitled to a decent quality of service and to housing which is appropriate to their needs as they see them. Even the Benefits Agency is said to be, 'conscious of the need to ensure that the service the customer receives is of an acceptable standard regardless of the customer's circumstances' (DSS 1992). Any other starting point is not good enough practice and it is also likely to prove ineffective; people who are 'placed' in accommodation which they feel has been inappropriately foisted on them tend to regain control of the situation by leaving.

Support for the moral right to decent housing can bring social workers into conflict with housing workers, who also have few resources; but this is an inevitable consequence of advocacy which may be all that social workers can realistically offer. Willingness to advocate and 'work the system', from a position of relative professional power, is valued by service users, even when it fails to produce material results; taking the issue seriously and trying seem to be what counts (Stewart and Stewart 1993a).

Collaboration is one of the holy grails of modern social policy: social workers and housing workers are constantly urged by the government to work together and provide a 'seamless service' of community care, or whatever. Of course this is desirable to a certain extent, in order to fulfil a public service duty to communicate efficiently between agencies, eliminate mutual hostilities and provide consistent information to the public. Beyond that, collaboration can become not only difficult (Arblaster *et al.* 1996; Arnold *et al.* 1993; Means and Smith 1996; SSI 1994) but also undesirable.

The holy grail of 'collaboration' can become a threat to good professional practice when clients' best interests, as jointly assessed with them, are compromised in order to protect harmonious inter-agency relations. I have been writing unashamed social work apologeties, but there is equal need for constructive housing apologies to point out the excluding potential of social work services. The presentation of a 'seamless' united front can be experienced as an impenetrable barrier by someone who has been denied a service, and that is one way in which both social workers and housing workers risk becoming key players in the process of social exclusion.

Within their own departments, social workers need to be aware of opportunities for championing service users' financial interests, even against the power of the purchasing manager. Six years after implementation of the Children Act 1989 there is evidence of underuse of its financial powers for giving money to families with children 'in need' (Association of Charity Officers 1997; Local Government Anti-Poverty Unit 1996). The tendency to offer any help in kind rather than cash implies moral judgement (Hyden 1996) and a lack of trust which disempowers poor families. There is no justification for meanness in giving financial assistance when it is within social workers' discretion, although internal agency policies on this issue might have to be challenged.

Similarly, there has been widespread reluctance by Social Services management to start implementing the Community Care (Direct Payments) Act 1996 which allows cash payments to disabled people who want to manage their own services. On the other hand, some departments have shown initiative in finding ways to help home care users who have to pay means tested charges for domiciliary services, by doing routine checks of benefit entitlement or mounting welfare rights take-up campaigns targeted at particular groups. Social workers in authorities which have not adopted this approach could sell the idea to purchasing managers with the argument that income can be raised for the department as well as service users by increasing their ability to pay higher charges (Alcock and Vaux 1997).

Benefits issues in the 1990s have not aroused the same passion among social workers as the Social Fund did at the end of the eighties (Stewart and Stewart 1993b), perhaps because of a general preoccupation with implementing major new legislation. Concerns about cash/care boundaries have a long history and social work responses to poverty and housing issues during the past three decades have been mixed and ambivalent (Becker 1997; Dowling 1997; Stewart and Stewart 1986; Trainor 1996). After its heyday in the late 1970s class-focused social work radicalism became sidelined, as Thatcherism took its toll and the discourse moved on; since then poverty has been virtually excluded from British debates about anti-discriminatory practice (Thompson 1993).

Conclusion

The broader theoretical context of social exclusion which I have been exploring in this chapter has important implications for social work practice and I have suggested ways that social workers may respond to the experience of social exclusion amongst service users. A rediscovery of poverty and homelessness by north American social work writers has generated analytical tools for re-integrating these issues into anti-discriminatory practice thinking. Starting from the radicals' premise that 'the personal is political', (Mullaly 1993, p.155) argues the relevance of social exclusion for social work ethics and methods. Social workers' individual practice necessarily has political ends: for conventional social work the political end is to maintain the status quo, and this is done by personalising social problems such as homelessness. Alternatively the political end for what he calls structural social work is to change the status quo and counter oppression, by always making connections between individual problems and their structural context. In practice this means moving beyond 'mere psychosocial manipulations' which pathologise service users. Understanding and being aware of structural reasons for private circumstances enables the social worker to communicate this information to the person and put their situation into perspective, thus reducing the guilt and self-blame (internalised oppression) which many people experience when they are homeless, in multiple debt or otherwise in extreme poverty. Following this analysis, social work is either part of the problem of social exclusion or part of its solution, there can be no middle way.

References

Alcock, P. and Vaux, G. (1997) 'Reconciling cash and care: home care charges and benefit checks in social services.' *British Journal of Social Work 27*, 499–513.

Arblaster, L., Conway, J., Foreman, A. and Hawtin, M. (1996) *Asking the Impossible? A Study of Inter-Agency Working to Address Housing, Health and Social Care Needs of People in General Needs Housing.* Bristol: Policy Press.

Arnold, P., Bochel, H., Broadhurst, S. and Page, D. (1993) *Community Care: The Housing Dimension.* York: Joseph Rowntree Foundation.

Association of Charity Officers (1997) *Charities Helping People in Need.* London: Association of Charity Officers.

Audit Commission (1986) *Making a Reality of Community Care.* London: HMSO.

Bebbington, A. and Miles, J. (1989) 'The background of children who enter local authority care.' *British Journal of Social Work 19*, 5, 349–368.

Becker, S. (1997) *Responding to Poverty. The Politics of Cash and Care.* London: Longman.

Biehal, N., Clayden, J., Stein, M. and Wade, J. (1995) *Moving On: Young People and Leaving Care Schemes.* London: HMSO.

Brown, K.S. and Ziefert, M. (1990) 'A feminist approach to working with homeless women.' *Affilia 5*, 1, 6–20.

Burrows, R. (1997a) *Contemporary Patterns of Residential Mobility in Relation to Social Housing in England.* York: Centre for Housing Policy, University of York.

Burrows, R. (ed) (1997b) *Homelessness and Social Policy.* London: Routledge.

Campbell, B. (1993) *Goliath: Britain's Dangerous Places.* London: Methuen.

Carlen, P. (1994) 'The governance of homelessness: legality, lore and lexicon in the agency-maintenance of youth homelessness.' *Critical Social Policy 14*, 2, 18–35.

Carlen, P. (1996) *Jigsaw: A Political Criminology of Youth Homelessness.* Buckingham: Open University Press.

Chapman, T. and Cook, J. (1988) 'Marginality, youth and government policy in the 1980s.' *Critical Social Policy 22,* 41–64.

Daly, G. (1996) *Homeless: Policies, Strategies and Lives on the Streets.* London: Routledge.

Dean, H. (1992) 'Poverty discourse and the disempowerment of the poor.' *Critical Social Policy 12,* 2, 79–88.

Dean, H. and Melrose, M. (1996) 'Unravelling citizenship: the significance of social security benefit fraud.' *Critical Social Policy 16,* 3, 3–31.

Dean, H. and Taylor-Gooby, P. (1992) *Dependency Culture: The Explosion of a Myth.* Hemel Hempstead: Harvester Wheatsheaf.

Dennis, N. (1997) *The Invention of Permanent Poverty.* London: Institute of Economic Affairs.

Department of the Environment (1977) *Housing Policy: A Consultative Document.* Cmnd.6851, London: HMSO.

Department of Social Security (1992) *Homeless Customers, Hostels, Residential Care and Nursing Homes: Procedures and Good Practice Guide.* London: HMSO.

Dowling, M. (1997) *Social Work and Poverty.* Aldershot: Avebury.

Downing-Orr, K. (1996) *Alienation and Social Support: A Social Psychological Study of Homeless Young People in London and in Sydney.* Aldershot: Avebury.

Driver, S. and Martell, L. (1997) 'New Labour's communitarianisms.' *Critical Social Policy 17,* 3, 27–46.

Field, F. (1989) *Losing Out: The Emergence of Britain's Underclass.* Oxford: Blackwell.

Fimister, G. (1995) *Social Security and Community Care in the 1990s.* Sunderland: Business Education Publications.

Fisher, K. and Collins, J. (eds) (1993) *Homelessness, Health Care and Welfare Provision.* London: Routledge.

Garside, P., Grimshaw, R.W. and Ward, F.J. (1990) *No Place Like Home: The Hostels Experience.* London: HMSO.

Golding, P. (ed) (1986) *Excluding the Poor.* London: Child Poverty Action Group.

Griffiths, S. (1996) *How Housing Benefit Can Work for Community Care.* York: Joseph Rowntree Foundation.

Hutson, S. and Liddiard, M. (1994) *Youth Homelessness.* London: Macmillan.

Hyden, L.C. (1996) 'Applying for money: the encounter between social workers and clients – a question of morality.' *British Journal of Social Work 26,* 843–860.

Ingram, M., Corning, A.F. and Schmidt, L.D. (1996) 'The relationship of victimization experiences to psychological well-being among homeless women and low-income housed women.' *Journal of Counselling Psychology 43,* 2, 218–227.

Jordan, B. (1996) *A Theory of Poverty and Social Exclusion.* Cambridge: Polity Press.

Jordan, B. (1992) *Trapped in Poverty? Labour-Market Decisions in Low-Income Households.* London: Routledge.

Kirby, P. (1994) *A Word from the Street: Young People Who Leave Care and Become Homeless.* London: Centrepoint.

Lister, R. (1990) *The Exclusive Society: Citizenship and the Poor.* London: Child Poverty Action Group.

Lister, R. (ed) (1996) *Charles Murray and the Underclass: The Developing Debate.* London: Institute of Economic Affairs.

Local Government Anti-Poverty Unit (1996) *In Kind...Or In Cash: Section 17 and Support for Children in Poverty.* Association of Metropolitan Authorities.

Mann, K. (1992) *The Making of an English Underclass.* Milton Keynes: Open University Press.

Marris, P. (1996) *The Politics of Uncertainty.* London: Routledge.

Means, R. and Smith, R. (1996) *Community Care, Housing and Homelessness Issues: Obstacles and Innovative Practice.* Bristol: Policy Press.

Morris, L. (1994) *Dangerous Classes: The Underclass and Social Citizenship.* London: Routledge.

Mullaly, R. (1993) *Structural Social Work.* Toronto: McClelland and Stewart.

O'Leary, J. (1997) *Beyond Help?* London: National Homeless Alliance.

Robinson, F. and Gregson, N. (1992) 'The "Underclass": a class apart?' *Critical Social Policy 12,* 1, 38–51.

Shaw, A., Walker, R., Ashworth, J. and Jenkins, S. (1996) *Moving Off Income Support: Barriers and Bridges.* DSS Research Report no.53, London: HMSO.

Shiner, M. (1995) 'Adding insult to injury: homelessness and health service use.' *Sociology of Health and Illness 17,* 4, 525–549.

Smith, D.J. (ed) (1992) *Understanding the Underclass.* London: Policy Studies Institute.

Social Services Inspectorate, Department of Health (1994) *Implementing Caring For People: Housing and Homelessness.* London: HMSO.

Squires, P. (1990) *Anti-Social Policy: Welfare Ideology and the Disciplinary State.* Hemel Hempstead: Harvester Wheatsheaf.

Stewart, G. and Stewart, J. (1986) *Boundary Changes: Social Work and Social Security.* London: Child Poverty Action Group and British Association of Social Workers.

Stewart, G. and Stewart, J. (1992) 'Social work with homeless families.' *British Journal of Social Work 22,* 3, 271–289.

Stewart, G. and Stewart, J. (1993a) *Social Work and Housing.* London: Macmillan.

Stewart, G. and Stewart, J. (1993b) 'The politics of the Social Fund: social security policy as an issue in central-local government relations.' *Local Government Studies 19,* 3, 408–430.

Stewart, J., Stewart, G., Smith, D., Forward, C. (1994) *Understanding Offending Behaviour.* Harlow: Longman.

Tomas, A. and Dittmar, H. (1995) 'The experience of homeless women: an exploration of housing histories and the meaning of home.' *Housing Studies 10,* 4, 493–515.

Thompson, N. (1997) *Anti-Discriminatory Practice.* London: Macmillan.

Trainor, B. (1996) *Radicalism, Feminism and Fanaticism: Social Work in the Nineties.* Aldershot: Avebury.

Vincent, J., Deacon, A. and Walker, R. (1995) *Homeless Single Men: Roads to Resettlement?* Aldershot: Avebury.

Walker, A. and Walker, C. (1997) *A Divided Society.* London: Child Poverty Action Group.

Wilkinson, R. (1996) *Unhealthy Societies: The Afflictions of Inequality.* London: Routledge.

Williams, R. and Avebury, K. (eds) (1995) *A Place in Mind: Commissioning and Providing Mental Health Services for People Who Are Homeless.* NHS Health Advisory Service, London: HMSO.

CHAPTER 4

Joint Planning
Why Don't We Learn From the Past?

Christine Oldman

The welfare role of housing has a long history. In their provider role housing agencies have accommodated various special needs' groups. Furthermore, through their statutory responsibility for homelessness, local authority housing departments have been centrally involved, almost whether they liked it or not, in welfare issues. There has always been considerable joint work between social service departments and housing organisations but this has generally, until the quite recent past, been at the individual case work level. This chapter has several aims. First, it documents a number of policy 'events' which have attempted to move housing into a more prominent role. It then looks at specific areas of housing and social care collaboration: needs assessment, the provision of services to homeless people, service provision to rural community care users and the delivery of adaptations. The final section offers an analysis and a critique of collaboration at the strategic level between housing and community care agencies through a review of the joint planning literature.

The slow process of getting housing into community care
The Wagner and Griffiths reports
It was with the rebirth of community care in the late 1980s that serious discussion on joint planning between housing and social services began. Previously housing had a very minimal role in the joint planning system established after the 1974 reorganisation of the NHS (NFHA/MIND 1989). In 1988 the Wagner Committee on residential care highlighted the importance of housing settings. Commentators

on the relationships between housing and social care have tended to pay rather less attention to Wagner than the slightly later Griffiths (1988) report *Community Care: An Agenda for Action*. However, Wagner had very much more to say about the role of housing settings in enhancing independence for frail and vulnerable people:

> We believe that people should be able to make a positive choice between different models of care, when they can no longer cope with life unaided. At present they are too often presented with a stark choice between remaining in the community and moving into residential care. We believe that if needs for services and accommodation are looked at separately, however, the range of choice for each individual can be vastly expanded. (Wagner 1988, p.3)

In the late 1980s, Wagner and Griffiths were both calling for an end to the 'perverse incentives' which had militated against the development of health and social care packages to support people in their own homes. The specifically housing-related implications of their recommendations to separate the funding and provision of accommodation services from the funding and provision of care services were not well thought through.

The housing world was in a mild state of uproar about what it saw as the almost total neglect of housing issues from Griffiths' analysis of the failures of community care over the years (Oldman 1988). Griffiths saw housing simply as the backdrop of community care; he also noticed, in passing, its wealth potential. He commented in optimistic tones on the number of home equity schemes around at the time, which, he felt, could be used to purchase care services. Griffiths seems to have completely ignored, or else did not have pointed out to him, the fact that Government's housing policies were a serious threat to his proposed reforms. A consistent cutting back on social housing programmes over the years necessarily adversely affects community care policies. However, although those interested in housing were outraged that housing was presumed to play such a minor role in the 'new' community care they did not present any serious analysis of what this role might be.

The White Paper

The first major event in an account of housing's integration into community care came with the publication of the White Paper *Caring for People* (DoH 1989). For the first time, in a publication emanating from the Department of Health, the importance of housing was stressed. It was described as being the foundation of community care and the key to independent living. One of the White Paper's central messages was that people with community care needs want to stay in their own homes; it highlighted specific housing interventions such as the then new Disabled Facilities Grant (DFG) and 'Staying Put' or 'Care and Repair' schemes which could make remaining in the community a realistic option. It also saw a role for specialist housing provision such as sheltered housing but argued that this should be targeted to those older people with care needs. Although the White Paper was not very prescriptive as to how collaboration between agencies should operate, it placed a great deal of emphasis on community care planning as the mechanism for setting out the strategic direction of the new policies. Although it argued that 'social services authorities will need to work closely with housing associations and other providers of housing of all types in developing plans for a full and flexible range of housing' (DoH 1989, p.25) there was no discussion of how to write housing authorities into any formal planning machinery.

Following the White Paper, the NHS and Community Care Act was passed in 1990 but not fully implemented until the 1st April 1993. Its particular relevance to this chapter is that it introduced a legal requirement for social service departments to consult with housing authorities when drawing up community care plans and to notify housing bodies if there appeared to be a housing need in an individual community care assessment (sections 46 and 47). In the first few years after the 1990 legislation was enacted a spate of policy guidance on how to integrate housing into community care was brought out.

The 1992 joint circular

In 1992 the Department of the Environment and the Department of Health published a joint circular on housing and community care. Although viewed in a much more negative light by housing commentators than its 1994 Scottish counterpart, the circular did urge housing authorities to develop housing strategies which involved liaison with social service authorities. It was roundly condemned for stating firmly that the new community care should not lead to more housing resources being made available but it discussed collaboration at the service delivery level.

The Scottish Circular (Scottish Office 1994) placed housing authorities more firmly centre stage in joint planning structures: 'the aim should be that housing bodies are involved in deciding on priorities, objectives and output targets, identification of needs, the determination of responsibilities, and the allocation and use of funds and other resources'. (Scottish Office 1994, 3.5.1)

Department of Health guidance and monitoring

In the early years after the publication of Wagner and Griffiths the impetus to get housing recognised seemed to come mainly from the housing side but it was voiced in a generalised, even rhetorical, manner. From around 1993, however, the Department of Health seized the initiative as the implications of planning and managing the new arrangements in the absence of appropriate and affordable housing were realised. The Community Care Support Force which had been charged with the task of assisting local authorities and health authorities in their implementation of the community care aspects of the 1990 Act produced *Integrating the Housing Agenda into Community Care* in 1993 (DoH 1993a). This was a remarkably detailed blueprint for getting housing on board. It went far beyond the blandness of previous policy statements and spelt out what housing's contribution was to community care and how it could be fully realised at both the planning and service delivery level. Its intended target audience was social service authorities. It presented four central arguments for why housing should be on social services' agendas:

1. in developing flexible packages of care, care managers must include appropriate housing as well as health and social care or the package will often fail

2. reducing reliance on residential care (the central aim of the new legislation) does not mean just the expansion of home care but also the provision of appropriate housing

3. housing has had a key role over a long period of time in accommodating and supporting vulnerable people in the community. Such low level support has a crucial role to play but social services must more formally recognise and support it

4. the principles of housing rights (security of tenure, privacy, consultation) mesh well with the core values of the new community care (user empowerment, needs-led assessment *etc*).

The Paper made a number of recommendations on how joint working between housing and health and social care agencies can become more formalised. It argued that reliance on the old joint planning mechanisms will leave housing agencies feeling marginalised and it made a number of suggestions about joint resource bidding strategies and about integrating housing, social services and health plans:

> ...it is important that the Community Care plan is not seen in isolation but as part of an integrated process which relates to the health authority's purchasing strategy, the housing department's local housing strategy and the Housing Corporation's Regional Strategy Statements. In this way different agencies can co-ordinate their planning processes and cycles. (DoH 1993b, 3.3)

The Support Force investigation also included the issue of homelessness in its remit (DoH 1993b). Homelessness is perhaps the social policy issue which most illustrates the difficulty of any attempt to distinguish between what is a housing responsibility and what is a social care responsibility. Put simply, homelessness is both a housing problem and social problem. Traditionally, community care is confined to 'priority groups': *the* physically disabled, *the* mentally ill, *the* elderly and people with learning disability. Homeless people have no room in this sort of compartmentalising. The Support Force's concern was that homeless people, particularly those suffering from drug or alcohol abuse, would be marginalised under the new arrangements. Before April 1993 homeless people living in housing provision registered under the Residential Homes Act could have their accommodation, care and support costs met through the single DSS benefit: the residential care allowance. In the Paper social services' departments were urged to develop their skills as purchasers and commissioners of a 'different sort of market', that is the market for homeless people with support needs. The Paper also drew attention to the difficulties in joint working caused by different legislative frameworks. Social Services provide services to people who are 'ordinarily resident' in their areas; homeless people must prove 'local connection'.

The 26th May 1993 Laming/Langlands letter (SSI/NHSME) to health and social services authorities which set out the DoH's expectations for 1993/4 included 'improving collaboration with housing authorities and agencies'. In 1994 the deliberations of a special monitoring study in 14 areas carried out jointly by the Social Services Inspectorate, National Health Service Management Executive and the

Department of the Environment was published (Department of Health 1994). The study investigated what progress had been made in implementing the Laming/Langlands exhortations. Although many instances of good practice were found, it concluded that generally housing was being sidelined and that there was a lack of shared vision, uncoordinated planning and commissioning systems and a lack of user and carer involvement.

Further joint guidance

Three years on from the DoH monitoring exercise the Departments of Health and Environment published *Housing and Community Care: establishing a strategic framework* (1997). This was a determined effort to prescribe what should be done at the strategic level to achieve co-ordination between housing, social services and health authorities. The Paper took note of the various policy changes since the publication of the 1992 circular, for example: developments in primary care, changes in the funding of special needs housing and the Housing Act 1996. Two potential obstacles to implementing joint strategies were not mentioned–they were compulsory competitive tendering in housing management and changes within housing benefit making the funding of housing support costs more difficult (Oldman, Quilgars and Oldfield 1996).

    The discussion above has shown that there has been, in recent years, no shortage of direction from central government to social services departments as well as to housing departments concerning the importance of collaboration. The main impetus has been from the Department of Health which is concerned that the central policy imperative of the community care changes - to reduce reliance on residential care–would be thwarted without the inclusion of housing in joint planning systems. In the early years of the changes at least, housing interests championed for an enhanced role in community care planning, in essence because they saw the legislative changes offering development opportunities at a time of a continued squeeze from the Department of Environment on capital resources. A number of specific areas of housing and care collaboration are assessed below, in terms of how well they measure up to central government prescription.

Assessing housing need

Part of the task of getting housing into joint planning has been to determine what the housing requirements of community care are. Traditional housing needs concepts, such as overcrowding, are not very helpful. Despite a stream of work on developing particular methodologies for doing this, progress in assessing the housing needs of community care users has been relatively limited. Some commentators (e.g. Means and Smith 1994) have argued that this is because housing's role has remained ill-defined and ambiguous. Allen's (1997) analysis, however, suggested that progress is limited because housing's role is 'politically inconsequential'; it is simply, as Griffiths himself had implied earlier, the backcloth of community care.

Watson's (Watson and Harker 1993) early research formulated an approach for determining the future demand for special needs housing. Housing need was defined by Watson in terms of anticipated moves from existing accommodation: for example, young adults with learning disability living in a parental home or patients suffering from chronic mental illness in NHS long stay provision. There are two sets of difficulties with such an approach. First, there is a strong commitment voiced by the Disability Movement (among others) to ordinary, non-specialist accommodation (Morris 1994). Such a perspective holds moves to specialist provision to be damaging to disabled people. Second, the policy imperative of both the DoE and the DoH is to contain the costs of the new community care by supporting people in their own homes. Resource commitment to mainstream or specialist provision is to be kept to a minimum. In later versions of her 'pathways' methodology Watson (Watson and Conway 1995; Watson 1996) attempted to assess the 'demand' for housing services delivered to people living at home such as adaptations, home improvement agency services and peripatetic warden services.

Despite this attention to 'at home' services, Watson's approach to assessing housing needs for community care users is conducted in isolation from the needs assessment carried out by other key players: health and social care purchasers. The guidance reviewed earlier in this chapter called for a joint approach to assessment. The 1992 circular discussed the need to employ a cost effective orientation to assessment, for example in what situations is a major adaptation (a 'housing' resource) more cost effective than extra hours of home support (an SSD resource)?

Similarly, the DoH 1994 monitoring exercise did not find extensive evidence of different agencies developing their individual plans collaboratively.

Means (1996) reported on research conducted for Avon County Council on assessing the housing needs of community care users which attempted to employ principles of empowerment and normalisation. He outlined key principles which should inform any 'special needs' housing survey. These included the following:

- housing and community care strategies must recognise the rights of people with disabilities to participate fully in society through such measures as implementing access standards in general needs housing

- needs assessment must also recognise the desire of people to have mainstream housing and support services rather than segregated 'special services'

- it is essential to get the right combination of appropriate housing and appropriate support; inadequate housing can undermine a support package and vice versa

- the concept 'appropriate housing' should be defined generously; offers of accommodation in locations away from people's support networks will not be perceived as appropriate

- finally, needs assessment and joint planning should involve a partnership with users.

Although needs assessment may now slowly be moving to an adoption of the principles employed by the Avon survey, Allen (1997) noted that adherence to them was tokenistic in the early days of implementation. Despite the rhetoric of the White Paper, progress on user involvement in joint planning is slow (Bewley and Glendinning 1994).

Homelessness and community care

Traditionally, homelessness and community care have been viewed as distinct areas: housing departments' legal responsibilities for homelessness diverted them from community care. Recently, however, as the summary of policy guidance above has shown, the two areas have been closely linked. Community care policies themselves have been implicated in an increase in homelessness. A number of commentators (Cohen and Thompson 1992; Scott 1993; Shanks and Smith 1992) have noted that the process of deinstitutionalisation has brought with it an increase in the visibility of homeless people with mental health problems.

The academic literature on joint working has focused on the relationship between health and social care organisations. Oldman (1997), in the context of an evaluation of the DoE's Section 73 programme to prevent and relieve single homelessness, explored joint working between housing departments and social services departments. She found that it was characterised by a great deal of activity at the referral and liaison level between organisations delivering services to homeless people but that it lacked a coherence at the strategic level. The disaggregation of homelessness into discrete categories such as priority/non-priority, special needs/ordinary; single/family impeded joint working and did a disservice to those who are without secure accommodation. Housing and social care agencies disagreed over definitions of vulnerability and hence disputes over relative responsibilities were an inevitability. Social services' departments complained that their clients were unable to access suitable accommodation but, equally, housing agencies argued that tenants were inadequately supported by health and social care agencies. In many areas within the study inter-agency fora had been established and these were making some progress in assessing local needs, reviewing existing provision and developing plans for future service provision. Nevertheless, there was considerably more scope in all the fieldwork sites to make better use of scarce resources. There were significant unmet needs at the same time as considerable overlap of services and provision.

Other writers have made similar comments about housing and social service dealings over homelessness. Prior discussed the problems of providing community care services to the severely mentally ill:

> Time and time again homeless people with mental health problems receive only short term help from psychiatric services, inadequate follow up and no improvement in their housing situations on discharge. It is a failure of joint working which is dangerous, wasteful of resources and within the power of authorities to substantially and rapidly improve. (Prior 1994)

However the SSI monitoring study (DoH 1994) reported a number of instances of good practice where joint housing and social service panels have come to a consensus on definitions of 'vulnerability' in deciding who should be entitled to help under the homeless legislation.

Service provision in rural areas

The special problems of integrating housing and community care in rural areas had been very much neglected until 1994 when the Housing Association Charitable Trust launched its report *Supported housing in rural areas* (Clark, 1994). The following key issues were identified:

1. national and local statutory agencies do not always collaborate effectively

2. there is insufficient information on rural housing and support needs and provision

3. traditional or urban models of housing and support provision are not always appropriate in rural areas

4. attitudes and organisational structures can discourage and prevent the sensitive development of services in rural areas.

The Scottish Office has examined the particular problems of delivering housing and community care to sparsely populated areas (Field and Oldman 1997). Provision can be very costly, particularly start-up costs. Housing providers are also reluctant to develop supported projects because they believe that the health and social care services necessary for maintaining a tenancy will not be available. Rural areas contain a range of needs and dependency levels but each in small quantities. Transport and travelling distances are often a major difficulty. Rural areas are not homogeneous and the housing and care needs of a 'deep' rural or island community may be different from those of a rural area a short driveaway from a town. However, the study found a number of instances of effective inter-agency working, particularly in the provision of flexible supported housing projects which were helping to avoid moves to residential care many miles away from users' supportive networks. There may be some opportunities in rural areas which would be more difficult to seize in the urban context. First, some rural communities are more close-knit and supportive. Innovation is not always imposed from above but comes about through locally-based surveys carried out by local people. Joint working can sometimes be easier because organisations are small scale and individuals within them can more easily make connections with different professionals. It can also be easier in the rural context to adopt a flexible approach to policies and procedures.

The study also looked at the issue of co-terminosity. Until recently in Scotland housing powers resided within second tier authorities. It has been believed that joint working between housing and social services is easier in unitary authorities. However, the study concluded that co-terminosity was only a minor factor in explaining the success or otherwise of joint working.

The provision of adaptations

Joint working between housing and social services is unavoidable as far as the provision of adaptations is concerned. Social services' departments have to confirm that a DFG, the main vehicle for funding adaptations, is necessary and appropriate'. The Department of Health has become increasingly active in trying to promote good practice in the planning and delivery of adaptation services to older and disabled people. Hospital discharge agreements are harder to keep in the absence, as is so often the case, of swift and effective adaptations. The problems of administering adaptations have been extensively documented (Heywood 1994; Heywood 1996; Mackintosh and Leather 1994; Pieda 1996). Adaptations illustrate graphically the issue of 'cost shunting' which is endemic in community care. The DFG is housing money; social services' spending on adaptations dramatically reduced with its introduction. In many areas there has been confusion and uncertainty over relative responsibilities towards the funding of adaptations. The funding of adaptations for disabled children is a particular victim of different legislative responsibilities. Although joint working between social services and housing is important as far as this group are concerned the legislative arena is the Children Act 1989. Disabled children are thus excluded from community care policies; however, joint working on adaptations derives from community care legislation (Heywood 1996). Other key difficulties which adversely affect joint working in this area are increasing cuts in home improvement resources and occupational therapist shortages.

A critique of joint working

The review above has shown that although some progress has undoubtedly been made at getting housing on board community care, there are a number of difficulties. This should not be a surprise: joint working failures, to borrow from Adrian Webb's famous phrase, have littered the policy landscape (Webb 1991). Webb was confining himself to joint working between health and social care agencies; adding a third statutory agency only compounds problems. Arnold *et al.* (1993) were very critical of early efforts to fit housing agencies into established joint planning structures; housing officers were 'bit part' players.

Hudson is representative of those who employ insights from organisational theory to explain why Government exhortations such as those in *Housing and Community Care: establishing a strategic framework* (DoH/DoE 1997) are highly problematic:

> From an agency's viewpoint, collaborative activity raises two main difficulties. First, it loses some of its freedom to act independently when it would prefer to maintain control over its domain and affairs. Second, it must invest scarce resources and energy in developing and maintaining relationships with other organisations when the potential returns on this investment are often unclear and intangible. (Hudson 1987)

It is clear that there are more obvious benefits to health and social care agencies of getting housing authorities to work with them than the other way round. For example, planning agreements containing housing departments' resource commitment to the delivery of adaptations are essential if reliance on NHS and residential provision is to be reduced. Housing, in turn, might gain development opportunities through collaboration but these will always be very limited.

The rapid organisational change that has affected all three statutory agencies has deflected them from working well together. Moreover, the new community care itself is inherently full of contradictions. On the one hand collaboration is stressed but on the other the purchaser provider split which has been implemented in different ways according to different timetables in all three sectors is a major obstacle. Housing associations, for example, who are major providers of housing and care services feel excluded from joint planning. Nocon sums up these problems:

> Until now providers have been part of the planning process contributing considerable expertise about needs and ways of meeting them. But how can their continued input be reconciled with the market system when those providers may be beneficiaries of the purchasing process. An increasing

amount of health authority business is already being conducted behind close doors for reasons of commercial confidentiality; there is a real contradiction between the new ethos of competition and the call for collaboration. (Nocon 1994, p.28)

The current author's work on joint working and homelessness (Oldman 1997) referred to earlier in the chapter graphically illustrates Nocon's analysis. Joint working relating to homelessness is characterised by (i) disputes about relative roles and responsibilities: 'what is a housing problem and what is a social care problem' and by (ii) competition for scarce resources. The chief executives of four major not-for-profit UK supported housing organisations in 1996 published a polemic designed to show that the failures of joint working are attributable to structural or institutional fault lines rather than poor communication or lack of experience of joint working (Harker *et al.* 1996).

Some commentators place an emphasis on values, ideology and professional differences in addition to more structural or organisational explanations for the failures of joint working. Nocon (1994) has argued that effective collaboration does not require all the agencies to share exactly the same set of values but it does require those values to be compatible. So often, however, values are not shared. There is a long history of enmity between housing and social workers. In evidence to the 1982 Barclay Committee on the future of social work the Institute of Housing wrote, 'Unfortunately, in many cases the working relationships between housing officers and social workers is not good...generally speaking they view each other with considerable scepticism' (BASW 1985).

More recently Franklin and Clapham (1997), defining the nature of the housing management task, have reported that housing staff feel that social work and housing management operate different cultures. They believed that social work involvement is with people as individuals with a right to live as they choose, regardless of the effect on others. Housing staff also felt that social workers' insistence on confidentiality could be a source of frustration.

Although she has not looked specifically at housing organisations Dalley's (1991) analysis of professional cultures, 'tribal ties' and lack of trust is particularly useful in explaining the relationships between housing and social services regarding the implementation of the community care changes. Nocon and Pleace (1997) employ a social services' perspective in a study of the housing needs of people with

physical disabilities. Joint working is flawed, they argue, because housing professionals are not in sympathy with social workers' increased emphasis on user-led
services. There is, however, criticism of this position from a number of quarters.
The independent living movement argue that social workers' commitment to no-
tions such as empowerment is lukewarm, for example (Oliver 1993). Housing professionals, as well, reject the view that housing values are not in line with
community care. Fletcher (1994) presents a persuasive argument that housing professionals are committed to community care because they are concerned about the
well-being of communities as well as individuals. Moreover he proposes that a
housing philosophy based on individual rights either through a tenancy agreement or through ownership of one's own home puts the user in a powerful position.

Finally, the chapter has shown that different values derive from different legislative responsibilities. For example, it has looked at conflicts in joint working with
homeless people about the interpretation of the different legal concepts 'ordinary
residence' and 'local connection' and at the difficulties for families of disabled children seeking to address their housing problems. The needs of disabled children are
met within Children Act legislation yet joint working to deliver adaptations to
people with disabilities goes on within a community care arena.

Conclusion

This chapter has documented the development of joint working between housing
and social services and shown that the impetus to get housing into the formal system of planning came from the relaunch of community care from the late 1980s
onwards. It has also illustrated this process through an examination of a number of
specific areas where collaborative working is taking place.

The key question with which this chapter must end is whether Allen's thesis
(1997) that housing's part in community care is technical, and thus subordinate,
will always hold true or whether progress will continue to be made in developing a
substantive and active role for it. Allen employed a sociological analysis to demonstrate the weakness of arguments which attempt to show that housing was slow to
come into community care because its role had not been understood or made explicit. Rather, he argued, housing is falsely associated with principles such as inde-

pendent living or normalisation. Community care is centrally concerned with reducing reliance on residential care. It pays only lip service to these concepts.

This chapter's conclusion, however, is that Allen (1997. C.f. Allen's contribution to this volume) is being unduly pessimistic. The boundaries between housing and social care are increasingly being questioned and negotiated by housing providers (Franklin and Clapham 1997). Housing management with the introduction of initiatives such as floating support (Morris 1995), despite the problem of funding support, is challenging the distinction between the technical role of housing and its social contribution. Allen is right in suggesting that the new community care is not about giving users real power over their lives. However, there is evidence that housing support workers and managers may collude with users to take forward with social services' bureaucrats the principles of user empowerment. Housing organisations are crossing the housing and care divide despite the efforts of Government departments to get them to return to being property managers. It is possible that housing providers and users will work more closely with social service purchasers to put in place user-led community care.

References

Allen, C. (1997) 'The policy and implementation of the housing role in community care: a constructionist theoretical perspective.' *Housing Studies 12*, 1, 85–110.

Arnold, P., Bochel, H., Broadhurst, S. and Page, D. (1993) *Community Care: the Housing Dimension.* York: Joseph Rowntree Foundation.

British Association of Social Work (1985) *Housing and Social Work.* Birmingham: BASW.

Clark, D. (1994) *Supported Housing in Rural Areas.* London: The Housing Association Charitable Trust.

Cohen, C.I. and Thomas, K.S. (1992) 'Homeless mentally ill and mentally ill homeless.' *American Journal of Psychiatry 149*, 816–821.

Dalley, G. (1991) 'Beliefs and behaviour: professionals and the policy process.' *Journal of Ageing Studies 5*, 2, 163–180.

Department of Health (1989) *Caring for People: Community Care in the Next Decade and Beyond.* London: HMSO.

Department of the Environment/Department of Health (1992) *Housing and Community Care,* Circular 10/92 and LAC (92) 12, London: HMSO.

Department of Health (1993a) *Integrating the Housing Agenda into Community Care.* Community Care Support Force.

Department of Health (1993b) *Community Care Services for Homeless People.* Community Care Support Force.

Department of Health (1994) *Housing and Homelessness: Report of the Community Care Monitoring Special Study*. October 1993–April 1994. Department of Health.

Department of Health and Department of Environment (1997) *Housing and Community Care: Establishing a Strategic Framework*. Wetherby: Department of Health Publications.

Field, J. and Oldman, C. (1997) *The Provision of Housing and Community Care in Rural Scotland*. Edinburgh; Scottish Office.

Fletcher, P. (1994) 'Housing and community care: from rhetoric and reality.' *Community Care Management and Planning 1*, 5, 138–147.

Franklin, B. and Clapham, D. (1997) 'The social construction of housing management.' *Housing Studies 12*, 1, 7–26.

Griffiths, R. (1988) *Community Care: Agenda for Action*. London: HMSO.

Harker, M., Kilgallon, W., Palmer, J. and Tickell, C. (1996) *Making Connections: Policy and governance for Community Care.*London: Special Needs Housing Association Group.

Heywood, F. (1994) *Adaptations: Finding Ways to Say Yes*. Bristol: School for Advanced Urban Studies.

Heywood, F. (1996) *Funding Adaptations: the Need to Co-operate*. Bristol: The Policy Press.

Hudson, B. (1987) 'Collaboration in social welfare: a framework for analysis.' *Policy and Politics 15*, 3, 175–182.

Mackintosh, S. and Leather, P. (1994) 'Funding and managing the adaptation of owner occupied homes for people with physical disabilities.' *Health and Social Care in the Community 2*, 229–239.

Means, R. (1996) 'From special needs' housing to independent living?' *Housing Studies 11*, 2, 207–229.

Means, R. and Smith, R. (1994) *Community Care: Policy and Practice*. Birmingham: Macmillan.

Morris, J. (1994) *Independent Lives: Community Care and Disabled People*. Basingstoke: Macmillan.

Morris, J. (1995) *Housing and Floating Support: A Review.* York: Joseph Rowntree Foundation.

National Federation of Housing Associations/MIND (1989) *Housing: the Foundation of Community Care*. London: NFHA.

Nocon, A. (1994) *Collaboration in Community Care in the 1990s*. Sunderland: Business Education Publications.

Nocon, A. and Pleace, N. (1997) 'Until disabled people get consulted: the role of occupational therapy in meeting housing needs.' *British Journal of Occupational Therapy 60*, 3, 115–122.

Oldman, C. (1988) 'More than bricks and mortar.' *Housing* June/July, 13–14.

Oldman, C. (1997) 'Working together to help homeless people: an examination of inter-agency themes.' In R. Burrows, N. Pleace and D. Quilgars (eds) *Homelessness and Social Policy*. London: Routledge.

Oldman, C., Quilgars, D. and Oldfield, N. (1996) *Housing Benefit and Service Charges*. London: The Stationery Office.

Oliver, M. (1993) 'Disability and dependency: a creation of industrial societies?' In J. Swain, V. Finkelstein, S. French and M. Oliver (eds) *Disabling Barriers: Enabling Environments*. London: Sage and Open University Press.

Pieda (1996) *An Evaluation of the Disabled Facilities Grants System.* London: HMSO.

Prior, C. (1994) 'Climb the mountain of community care.' *Inside Housing,* September, 14–15.

Scottish Office (1994) *Community Care: the Housing Dimension.* Circular Env 27/1994, Circular SW 7/1994, Circular NHSME (1994)79. Edinburgh: HMSO.

Scott, J. (1993) 'Homeless and mental illness.' *British Journal of Psychology 162,* (March).

Shanks, N. and Smith, S. (1992) 'Public policy and the health of homeless people.' *Policy and Politics 20,* 1, 35–46.

Social Services Inspectorate/National Health Service Management Executive (1993) *Laming/Langlands letter, Community Care Implementation and Monitoring.* Leeds: SSI/NHSME.

Wagner Report (1988) *Residential Care: A Positive Choice.* London: HMSO.

Watson, L. (1996) *Housing Needs and Community Care: the Housing Pathways Pilot Programme.* London: NFHA.

Watson, L. and Conway, T. (1995) *Homes for Independent Living: Housing and Community Care Strategies.* Coventry: Chartered Institute of Housing.

Watson, L. and Harker, M. (1993) *Community Care Planning: a Model for Housing Need Assessment with Reference to People with Learning Disabilities.* London: NFHA.

Webb, A. (1991) 'Co-ordination, a problem in public sector management.' *Policy and Politics 19,* 4, 29–42.

CHAPTER 5

Post-Modernism and Knowledgeable Competence
Social Work, Housing Management and Community Care Needs

Chris Allen

The 'user-centred' rationale that ostensibly underpins community care has been associated with broader patterns of social change, in particular the post modern emphasis on the salience of individual experience (Parton 1996). This has enervated certitude in the efficacy of insular stocks of specialist knowledge (such as bio-medical knowledge and social work knowledge) because they are seen to predominate over the experiential perspective of the individual. Conversely, enhanced emphasis has been given to the notion of *generic empiricism* because it is considered better equipped to unearth the multifarious and contingent nature of individual experience.

A logical derivative of post modernism's emphasis on experience over knowledge has engendered the belief that *generic empiricists* working at the interstices between organisations (rather than *knowledgeable specialists* operating within modern structural forms) should conduct multi-disciplinary investigations into the unpredictable particularism of personal problems. That is to say, a 'holistic' conception of individual experience cannot emerge in the absence of joint assessment approaches to empirical investigation—or at least, so the argument goes. Indeed, the notion that 'joint work' is 'good work' has become so reified that the housing, social work and health studies literature about community care is now preoccupied with identifying measures that facilitate more effective joint working practices.

The purpose of this chapter is not to reinvent the wheel by asking the question 'how can joint working practices be improved in order to ensure that holistic assessments occur?' Rather, it takes a step backwards from the accepted assumptions that sustain the post modern culture of 'joint working'. To this end, the chapter examines the extent to which post modernism's waning confidence in specialist knowledge, in favour of an emphasis on *generic empiricism,* has engendered an actual or rhetorical focus on the salience of *individual experience.* In doing so, it is concerned with two more specific questions. These are:

1.   to what extent do *knowledgeable social workers* and *generic housing managers* possess the competence to incorporate individual experience into their housing needs assessments?

2.   to what extent should social workers therefore be required to engage in joint work with housing managers in order to engender an appropriate housing need assessment outcome?

The chapter is based partly on the findings of a recent study of how social workers and housing managers assessed housing need in a community care context. The data that are used from field work conducted in social services authorities have been extracted from interviews undertaken with social workers who obtained their knowledgeable competence from the CQSW or DipSW. (Interviews undertaken with CSS qualified social workers, unqualified social workers and social work assistants have been omitted from the analysis). The data that are used from the field work conducted in housing authorities and housing associations have been extracted from interviews undertaken with housing managers and support workers. However, although the chapter draws on data from this specific project, its ultimate aim is to critically examine and illuminate the implications of a range of research for social work practice.

Post-Modernism, joint working and the 'social role' of housing management

Post-Modernism and the emergence of a 'joint working' culture

In conditions of modernity, personal problems were solved by social workers, medical professionals and others through the 'rational' application of an insular stock of specialist knowledge. However, post modernism's emphasis on the notion that personal problems are located in a broad range of highly particular and contingent factors has enervated certitude in such approaches. In doing so, this has led to the re-emergence of empirical approaches that incorporate broadly based conceptions of the problem and thus focus on the 'total life' of the personal.

This has engendered two notable consequences. First, the need to infuse professionals with a *knowledgeable* competence in specialist areas of the social or natural sciences has been questioned. Rather, emphasis has been placed on the development of training courses that are designed to imbue members of the caring occupations (such as social work, district nursing and community psychiatric nursing) with a broad base of generic *skills* (DoE 1997; Jones 1996; Payne 1995; Sibeon, 1991a, 1991b; Webb 1996). Second, since the problems of the personal are now seen to reside in an unpredictable plethora of factors, functionaries based in insular occupations (such as social work, district nursing and so on) are no longer considered to possess the knowledgeable competence or resources to solve these problems. To this end, it is has been argued that personal problems should be assessed through joint working practices where skills and resources can be brought together to engender a 'holistic' approach (Clarke 1996; Hallett 1991).

The extent to which the notion that joint work is good work (and the converse contention that insular approaches produce incomplete outcomes) has become accepted as 'common sense' is staggering. The issues that stem from the concept dominate debates within academic and practice journals. In doing so, the hegemony enjoyed by this claim has constrained legitimate issues for empirical investigation. Researchers are now requested on a regular basis (e.g., by the Department of the Environment, Department of Health, Joseph Rowntree Foundation, Scottish Homes, Welsh Local Government Association, Local Government Management Board) to establish the extent to which joint work is being conducted, to examine the barriers which hinder joint approaches to work, and to identify successful models of inter-agency collaboration. Work has yet to be conducted with the explicit purpose of examining whether joint working is efficacious, or even relevant.

The culture of joint working and community care assessments

During the initial stages of community care implementation, social work and housing authorities were swamped by a deluge of governmental guidance. Based on the axiom that 'joint work' is 'good work', each promoted the importance of joint planning, joint training and joint assessments and advised that the

> ...social services department...notify the local housing authority and invite [it] to assist in [community care] assessment. (Welsh Office 1992)

> ...referral procedures and the timing of the input from the different housing bodies needs to be developed and agreed locally. (Welsh Office 1991)

As tends to occur with major legislative changes, a new policy analysis industry was created almost overnight. Researchers were asked to undertake an ever expanding series of investigations which (paying due consideration to the large degree of support that the concept of joint working enjoys) was designed to examine the extent to which actual occurrence coalesced with conjectured occurrence. Predicating their investigations on the supposition that a housing management input into community care assessments represented the prerequisite of an effective outcome (Arnold 1992; Arnold *et al.* 1993), researchers duly set about examining the extent to which joint assessments were taking place. They then concluded *en masse* that the ubiquitously apparent exclusion of housing practitioners from the assessment process indicated that housing needs were not being adequately assessed. These methodologically dubious 'findings' have since provided housing researchers with the ammunition to engage in a stream of ill-informed polemics suggesting that

- because standardised procedures, designed to ensure the input of housing practitioners in community care assessments (e.g. joint assessment forms, housing need triggers in assessment forms, protocols for joint assessment and referral, liaison officers to conduct joint assessments and deal with referrals) had not been established between social work authorities and housing organisations, the logical derivative suggested that housing needs were not being addressed (Allen, Clapham and Franklin 1995; Allen and Walker 1994; Arnold *et al.* 1993; Arnold and Page 1992; Clapham 1994a; Clapham and Franklin 1994b; Leigh 1994; Macfarlane and Laurie 1996).

- in the absence of such joint working, social workers lacked the knowledgeable competence to assess housing needs and, as a result, inappropriate options were being pursued which reflected the institutionalising ethos of social work. (Arnold *et al.* 1993; Clapham 1994; Watson 1994)

I have already suggested that an uncritical acceptance of the notion that joint work is coequal to good work is indicative of the methodological paucity of these findings. However the coterminous proposition that social work is underpinned by an institutional ethos highlights an additional weakness. This is the substantive circumvention that characterises the community care research undertaken within the discipline of housing studies (Allen 1997a). Circumvention involves a preoccupation with substantive issues present in the researcher's host discipline (in this case, housing studies) and an unwillingness to engage with relevant community care issues present in other peripheral disciplines (such as social work or health care studies). In housing and community care studies, substantive circumvention has engendered two notable consequences. On the one hand it has encouraged housing researchers to adopt the anti-social work rhetoric of ill-informed housing managers. Housing managers tend to present interviewers with malevolent images of social workers who, equipped with a *specialist knowledge*, think they 'know best' and thus impose their 'professional orthodoxy' onto older and disabled people. Housing managers find it hard to resist painting a picture of their social work colleagues as incompetent functionaries who lack the technical expertise to assess housing need. On the other hand, substantive circumvention has encouraged housing researchers to present us with an benign view of the housing manager. This picture is predicated on the notion that housing managers are 'technical experts' who, untainted by 'professional orthodoxy', are unique in possessing the skills to act as advocates and as such, are able to transcend the temptation to stereotype need (see Arnold *et al.* 1993).

To ensure that housing and community care needs are 'properly' assessed, and without recourse to 'professional orthodoxy', a number of researchers have suggested that a standard assessment form should now be devised. It is argued that the standard structure of these forms will ensure that housing need is 'holistically' assessed by providing social workers and housing managers with a comprehensive sequence of generic questions to guide their empirical investigations (Arnold *et al.* 1993; Atkinson 1995). This is a recommendation to which the British Council of Organisations of Disabled People (BCODP) now subscribes. Indeed, the BCODP have gone so far as to produce a suggested 'housing assessment format'. This consists of an expansive sequence of closed format (i.e. tick box) housing need questions that empirically focus on an expanse of generic issues (see Macfarlane and Laurie 1996).

In the remainder of this chapter, I challenge the veracity of discourses which construct social workers as demonic incompetents and housing managers as enlightened competents. In doing so, I will demonstrate that a commitment to generic empiricism, which housing researchers believe to be the panacea to the vexatious question of the best way to ensure that a 'holistic' assessment of housing need is conducted, neither facilitates the primacy of the 'user voice' in the assessment encounter, nor transcends stereotypical formulations of need.

From a rhetorical to a cultural approach to Post-Modernism and knowledgeable competence

I have suggested that the notion that 'joint work' is commensurate with 'good work' (and the associated idea that a 'holistic' housing needs assessment requires the input of a housing practitioner) is spurious. That this idea has attained widespread credence is indicative of the theoretical paucity and substantive circumvention of community care research undertaken within housing studies (Allen 1997a). It is now therefore necessary to take a step backwards from the post modern rhetoric of 'holism' and 'diversification' that has hitherto been accepted at face value.

In doing so, there is a need to venture beneath the surface of post modern rhetoric in order to unearth and question the intricacies of its occurrence. To achieve this we first need to accept that 'housing need' is a social construct and to identify the 'housing need' hegemony. From this, the cultural function of the housing manager (who determines housing need in individual cases and sequentially rations housing to individuals) can be established. This provides a control measurement against which the appropriateness of the housing managers community care assessment practices can be examined. From this, an answer can then be found to the question of more general concern: 'to what extent is joint working relevant, if at all?'

Housing management, housing need and 'objective identification'

The constitution of a housing problem is a social construct that emerges and becomes consigned over time as a result of the discourses and discursive practices of politicians, housing administrators, housing market interests and their collaborators in housing research (Kemeny 1992). Two 'historical episodes' identified the components that are now generally considered to constitute a 'housing problem':

1. Charles Booth's *The Life and Labour of People in London* (1892), Seebohm Rowntree's *A Study of Town Life* (1902) and his subsequent studies of poverty in York between 1900 and 1950 were seminal and canonical works in establishing 'housing conditions' (such as 'overcrowding', 'dampness' and so on) as a major cause of ill health (Joseph Rowntree Foundation 1954).

2. Based on the demand side strategies of cost control and supply side strategies of dwelling provision, the incipient housing legislation of the late 19th and early 20th century established the principle that housing need should be framed in terms of the economics of supply and demand (Malpass and Murie 1990).

This being so, contemporary housing need is measured in terms of the gap between the demand for, and supply of, dwellings that coalesce with environmental health standards (see Holmans n.d.; Whitehead and Kleinman 1992). To this end, contemporary housing managers receive a technical and administrative training (Provan and Williams 1991). This training emphasises the use of objective indicators, such as 'amenities', 'space standards', and 'number of rooms', that can be 'read off' with calculable ease in order to establish housing need (Spicker 1993). The degree to which these objective indicators constitute an uncontroversial understanding of a 'housing problem' is in evidence by the extent to which legitimate political debate is circumscribed to technical arguments about how objective standards should be measured.

Formal housing management approaches to assessment

In conducting housing needs assessments, housing managers are guided by the section on 'special needs' in the arduous *Housing Management Standards Manual* (Chartered Institute of Housing 1996a, 1996b). Indeed, an entire document known as the *Care in the Community Housing Management Procedural Framework,* has been produced in Scotland to enable housing managers to 'deal with' the assessment of 'special housing needs' (Scottish Homes 1995). These documents promote a routine approach to producing results that are consistent with pre-defined standards. In many cases housing organisations have responded to such guidance by introducing sections on 'special needs' within mainstream housing application forms or by establishing separate 'special needs' assessment forms.

Housing need assessment forms tend to follow a highly structured format. On special housing needs assessment forms (which tend to be completed by the applicant, in the absence of the housing manager) older and disabled people are expected to express their needs by providing yes/no responses and, 'if appropriate', a narrative answer of no more than two or three lines to impersonal and laconic questions such as:

- Main reason why current accommodation inappropriate?

- Care and support currently offered to applicant?

- Applicant's specific future requirement?

- Areas most appropriate for rehousing and reasons?

On these forms, little interest is shown in the 'total life' of the person (i.e. their biographical life and social situation). To this end, housing managers endeavour to ensure that face-to-face contacts with 'clients' are kept to a minimum. Rather, the housing manager's interest in housing need is confined to technical factors and indicators that can be 'read off' assessment forms in an objective fashion. Indeed the 'objective identification' of need is considered to be so important that 'subjective expressions' of need, and the variability of outcomes that this implies, are regarded as anathema to good housing management practice, despite the emphasis given to particularism in the community care legislation:

> I think my role is there to ensure a consistency of approach...You need a consistent approach, because where before people who had special needs had to apply to 7 different teams they could be treated in 7 different ways. Now we don't have that. (Housing Manager)

> It's all terribly fair. It's all done by the book. There is the smallest amount of discretion by the assessment officer...[but]...basically everything is done desperately above board. (Housing Manager)

When housing need has been 'objectively identified', the medical officer then requests further information pertaining to the intricacies of the housing applicant's 'medical condition'. This information is usually produced by the applicant on a self completion assessment form, by answering more specific questions, such as:

- What is your medical condition?
- What treatment are you receiving?
- Please give the names of your medicine?
- What is your disability?

In each case, the applicant is expected to provide tick box answers and, if appropriate, an accompanying textual explanation of no more than a couple of lines. From this, the 'medical officer' determines the extent to which the 'expressed' need is a genuine need. The medical officer then provides priority points to 'genuine' applicants and recommends a course of action (that might conflict with the expressed wishes of the housing applicant) to ensure that their genuine housing needs are addressed in what she considers to be an 'appropriate' manner. Since medical officers prefer 'never [to] meet clients' and to 'stay out of it as much as possible', in order to 'retain the objectivity of the assessment process' and avoid being 'manipulated', this involves the utilisation of their 'medical expertise' to read between the lines of what is said on medical assessment forms.

> We also ask them to supply any pertinent information which may help their cause...Usually, if I can look at the medication it will back up or not the claim of the individual...The medical things help me to reach some sort of decision. (Medical Officer)

To this end, the medical expertise of the peruser is used as the benchmark to judge the answers that are given to the questions that are asked. This being so, legitimacy is only given to issues that medical officers (rather than housing applicants) consider to be salient. So, in the above quotation, the 'pertinent information' that would 'help their cause' would be assessed according to whether medical treatment was being received. The provision of an answer that was acceptable in the eyes of this medical officer would then back up the claim of the individual.

Notably, social workers considered this housing management function to represent an abhorrent form of practice. Indeed, so much so that when the contribution of the medical officer was explained, social workers demonstrated a bemusement with the function. The 'objective' medical points system was considered to be offensive for treating people as 'liars' and for medicalising and thus distorting the problems of older and disabled people:

> Well she's [the medical officer] insinuating that [what the client says] is lies isn't she. I think its terrible. You can't tell by what somebody's written on a form...just by reading a few lines. That's like us trying to do an assessment over the phone isn't it. Trying to write an assessment from a letter that was sent to us. (Social Worker)

Informal housing management approaches to assessment

In addition to this formal approach to assessment, the housing problems of older and disabled people are also assessed on an informal (face-to-face) basis. This occurs where generic or special needs housing managers conduct assessment visits prior to an allocation being made, or when the problems of existing tenants are encountered 'on their rounds'. The advent of this visiting function represents the manifestation of a recognition that a 'social role' should be incorporated within the scope of housing management. This poses the question of whether it is appropriate for housing managers to perform a social role; in particular one involving the assessment of 'special' housing needs. Hitherto, housing researchers have asserted the pressing need for housing managers to perform this social role at the interface with social work in order to ensure that 'special' housing needs are 'properly' assessed (Allen and Walker 1994; Clapham and Franklin 1994a, 1994b). However, since I am arguing that such assertions lack empirical foundation, it is necessary to provide a critical examination of the extent to which 'social' housing management practice does ensure that special housing need is properly assessed.

Let us therefore consider how the historical development of this social role has shaped modern housing management practice at its contemporary interface with social work. Two historical episodes have shaped the contemporary nature of this social role. First, the purpose of the social role established by Octavia Hill was to uphold the moral well-being of her tenants. This involved the creation of 'good tenants' who kept a good house and paid their rent on time (Spicker 1993). Second, during the slum clearance programmes of the 1920s and 1930s, the Women Housing Estate Managers elaborated the 'social role' by incorporating within it the social work methods of the Charity Organisation Society (Malpass and Murie 1990). However, despite incorporating COS social work methods, the 'social role' remained imbued with a moral ethos. This was because the COS favoured 'casework' theories of pathological decrepitude that endorsed the prevailing moral and social order (Hopkins 1996; Jones 1996).

Responding to the introduction of community care in the early 1990s, the Chartered Institute of Housing (CIH) has again argued that there is a need to re-incorporate a social role within the housing management function. However, in doing so it has, paradoxically, failed to make any effort to equip housing management students with the knowledge to enable them to perform it. In particular, the university courses which the CIH validates, in order to constitute what passes for 'housing knowledge', do not provide students with a critical understanding of contemporary social work theories. This is because the CIH prefers the skills of the modern housing manager to be derived from 'technocratic' disciplines such as architecture, engineering, building technology, law, public administration and management (Provan and Williams 1991). Thus, with few rules and resources to draw upon other than the 'common sense' that exists 'out there', and their own personal experiences, this unsurprisingly creates unreflexive housing managers who adopt moralistic approaches reminiscent of Octavia Hill.

> I see myself as the person *telling them how to be a tenant ... being a good tenant...* I see if the place has been cleaned ever in the few months that they've been there and I do try to *check up on them.* (Housing Support Worker; emphasis added)

Indeed, this imperative to create 'good tenants' recently acted as the stimulus for the Housing Corporation and Housing for Wales to provide housing associations with Special Needs Management Allowance funding, and for Scottish Homes to devise a special needs allowance package. The purpose of this source of funding is to enable housing associations to employ support workers with a specific remit to provide 'special needs' tenants with 'advice with regard to living in the house' (Scottish Homes 1993: 28). This normalising approach to providing tenants with 'support' contrasts with the contemporary social work approach which, informed by a sociological appreciation of normalcy and deviance, emphasises the right of tenants to pursue lifestyles that are different.

> ...he was sleeping on the settee and wearing the same clothes, his hair was long and matted so he wasn't looking after himself so I thought the time has come for some intervention (Housing Support Worker)

...the difference between us [and housing managers] is to do with risk management. What are the different perspectives I've got? Other people may have gone into a situation, including occupational therapists, and say 'this is terrible. This person shouldn't be on their own. They shouldn't be living like this'. Maybe the house is messy or untidy...and we, I think, to them [housing managers] are very laid back you know with the risk management...and all kinds of things and we'll come back and say 'well, I've had a look at that and we think its OK'. (Social Worker)

This social work approach is characterised by the manner in which it takes account of 'subjective expressions' of housing need rather than 'objective indicators' of housing need. Indeed, subjective expressions of need are considered to be so important that they are often pursued to extreme lengths, even where this involves maintaining older and disabled people in housing situations that could be 'objectively' considered to be unhealthy and dangerous.

I mean people have the choice and that's the way they want to live. If they are struggling with the facilities they have, maybe an outside toilet is an issue, if they couldn't work around that, they say, 'no, we want to live here' then I would look at ways around it...Some people are happy with what they have got, or maybe not what they've got but want to stay living where they are and making the best of what they've got. (Social Worker)

Nevertheless, it would be wrong to blame an institutional bias towards *training* for the theoretical paucity of housing *education*. Those who have been involved in teaching housing practitioners will be familiar with Gurney's (1991) complaint that the 'theoretical bits' of housing courses are frequently disliked and dismissed as irrelevant. Indeed, although community care is considered to be an interesting diversion from the mundane requirement to learn about the technical aspects of housing policy and practice, housing students demonstrate an abject lack of interest in the history and sociology of the policy. They often want to be told about the everyday problems that community care will present to them in their future careers, and about the resources that will be available to enable them to 'deal with' these problems. That is to say, there is a fetishism with the technocratic intricacies of problem solving, but a lack of interest in the wider context within which housing management performance takes place and of the implications that these performances might have. Both of these are important points and should be addressed in turn.

THE TECHNOCRATIC FETISHISM

Seminars with housing students are frequently dominated by the notion that 'problem tenants', who fail to live up to the standards expected of the 'good tenant', should be 'dealt with' through technocratic methods such as eviction. Spicker (1993) notes that this typifies the modern housing manager who puts a misplaced faith in technical solutions (such as the sanction of eviction against tenants), and who is simply unable to understand theoretically the (discriminatory, oppressive and socially controlling) impact that his practices have. Indeed, the following situation, in which a 'difficult tenant' is denied re-access to housing (because he previously failed to measure up to what housing managers considered to constitute a 'good tenant'), will be recognised by social workers as an all too familiar occurrence:

> *We've got one* [sic] at the moment which is going to be quite a hard one to resolve. Someone who in their past lives [i.e. previous tenancies] have been terribly disruptive and are well known to seven area teams and she is currently homeless. What she is requesting is in the areas where she is previously known and the area managers are not prepared to rehouse her given her history. (Special Needs Housing Officer)

Whilst this is interesting in itself, the language used here itself provides a further insight into the disjunctive assessment approaches of social workers and housing managers. When citing examples of situations in order to elucidate a more general point for the researcher, social workers usually talk about older and disabled people in first name terms. Housing managers, on the other hand, tend to refer to 'their' tenants by using impersonal terms such as 'case'. If nothing else, this highlights housing managers' limited interest in solving inconvenient problems, which are simply seen as a categories to be 'dealt with' through technocratic methods. Even where housing support workers engage with tenants on an informal basis, and are not subjected to the requirement to impose formal organisational classifications upon the situation, the individual is categorised and seldom treated as a person with problems that are highly particular and contingent:

I decide if they're going to be sort of A, B, C, D, or E's and how long they are going to need my support...It's purely my own little itty bitty categorisation for my own benefit...Just to make my life a bit easier. (Resettlement Housing Manager)

THE CONTEXT OF THE HOUSING MANAGEMENT PERFORMANCE

Housing students' lack of interest in the context of their performances is widely reflected in the practice of those who have been through the housing education system. In contrast to social workers who, I will argue later, recognise and endeavour to mediate reflexively the oppressive consequences of their function, housing managers seldom reflect upon or even recognise their role in enforcing normalcy and social control. Conversely, housing managers almost always consider themselves to be 'philanthropic' and 'magnanimous', and believe their interventions to represent the enlightened benevolence of an occupation that always endeavours to be 'helpful' - even when the function involves the overt imposition of social control:

I'm not a social worker. I'm a housing professional, but my job does have some social implications in that I'm actually concerned...about the social well-being of my re-settlements...*whether they're being good tenants.* (Housing Support Worker; emphasis added)

I try to be helpful and reiterate what the council says [about standards and behaviour] in a friendly sort of jolly way. You can get so much over to people if you don't come over too heavy handed. (Housing Support Worker)

Let us briefly recall what has been said up to now. I have noted that housing need hegemonies set the parameters within which personal problems are assessed and measured by housing managers. In Britain, the housing need hegemony supposes an empirical reliance on 'objective indicators' and has manifested itself in the emergence of a housing management practice that is preoccupied with the practical task of 'doing' and the technocratic training of knowing 'how to do it'. Unsurprisingly, this system is insensitive to subjective expressions of housing need which is instead objectively identified and then stereotyped into pre-defined categories. This is despite the introduction of community care, which now supposes need to be highly particular and contingent.

Nevertheless, the re-emergence of the social role has provided an opportunity to introduce more flexibility into the housing management method. Unfortunately however, there continues to be a general lack of interest in developing a sociological appreciation of contemporary social work methods amongst housing practitioners. To this end, housing managers have been left to conduct their social role according to the logic acquired from the 'common sense' that exists 'out there' and through personal experiences gained 'on the job'. This being the case, housing managers tend to prescribe solutions that can at best be considered to be inappropriate and, at worst, controlling and oppressive.

Social work knowledge and the assessment of housing need

In order to examine whether social workers possess enough knowledge to define the housing needs of older and disabled people, there is a need to pose the cantankerous question, 'what is (the nature of) social work?' Broadly speaking, social work *education* can be characterised by its historically fluid theoretical understanding of the relationship between the individual and society (Howe 1987; Jones 1996; Payne 1991; Sibeon 1991a, 1991b; Webb 1996). At its inception, the 'casework' method constituted the social work 'stock of knowledge'. Despite the later transfer of responsibility for social work education, from the Charity Organisation Society to a social science base in the universities, little changed because the social work academy was unique in failing to engage with radical sociology until the 1970s (Jones 1996; Webb 1996). This unique reluctance to engage with radical sociology occurred because psychoanalytic theories of casework served the purpose of creating the unified stock of knowledge that sustained social work's claims to the status of a profession (Hopkins 1996; Jones 1996). In addition to this, casework problematised the personal rather than society and, as such, was efficacious in 'making safe' the social worker's certainty that her activities were legitimate (Jones 1996).

More recently, Jones (1996) has suggested that, since social work continues to problematise, the personal, older and disabled people are disregarded, not listened to and, ultimately, do not count. However, the extent to which this can be considered to constitute a fair exposition of contemporary social work practice must be contested. First, the notion that the social work academy's failure to engage with critical social theory distinguishes it from other applied academic disciplines should be challenged. Second, the accuracy of the contention that theoretical social work encourages the total oppression of clients should also be challenged.

Social work and critical social theory – a special case?

According to Jones (1996), the conservatism that characterised the social work academy, prior to the 1970s, resulted directly from its focus on psychoanalytic theories. This, he argues, involved a failure to engage with critical social theory in order to 'make safe' social work education and practice from the uncertainty that its central knowledge base (i.e. casework theory) lacked legitimacy. However, whilst the evidence for this is compelling, it also raises the question of whether this strategy to 'make safe' is really unique to social work. I would suggest that the answer must be no. This tendency to 'make safe' well developed 'stocks of knowledge' is characteristic of a plethora of disciplines. One recent example is provided by Allen (1997a) who has criticised 'radicals' in the field of disability studies for becoming fixated with structuralist sociology. Here, 'making safe' has involved a reticence to engage with the 'middle range' sociologies of the body and sociologies of the emotions, in order to protect the canonical integrity of the 'social model of disability' which rejects any form of methodological individualism. In addition to this, social work is no different from other disciplines in seeking out theoretical knowledge from apparently obvious sources. Thus, whilst for housing studies, the obvious has incorporated political science, economics and a recent engagement with sociology (Allen and Gurney 1997), in social work the obvious, for a long time, involved a concern with psychoanalysis.

In considering the unique case of social work, recognition must also be given to the 'temporal slippage' that exists between theoretical developments and their utilisation within the applied disciplines. So, whilst Milliband and Poulantzas' debate on the state emerged in the late 1960s, these theoretical ideas did not infuse the applied disciplines until much later. Indeed, if social work is 'special', this is because *social work students* engaged with radical sociologies as early as the *early* 1970s and, in doing so, were instrumental in establishing a radical curriculum for the CQSW (Hopkins 1996; Jones 1996). This compares with housing studies whose *research constituency* did not engage with structural Marxism until the *late* 1970s and the *students* of which continue to demonstrate reticence towards critical social theory. Indeed, had it not been for the current CCETSW strategy of stripping social work courses of their theoretical content (Hopkins 1996; Howe 1991; Jones 1996; Sibeon 1991a, 1991b), there is little doubt that contemporary social work education would now be informed by a concern with the 'trendy' ideas of Giddens and Foucault which have only recently found their way into the applied disciplines on any notable scale.

So, it could be said that social work is not a 'special' case that can be distinguished from other applied social sciences. If anything, social work engaged with radical structural sociologies before many other disciplines (the most notable being housing studies). Indeed, the overt concern of social workers with the structural causation of personal problems led the CCETSW, as early as 1975, to contend that

> the education they [social workers] receive makes them difficult employees more concerned to change the 'system' than to get on with the job. (CCETSW 1975, quoted in Jones 1996)

Social work, housing need and 'subjective expression'

There has been a vigorous debate concerning the extent to which social theories are used in social work practice (Brennan 1973; Barbour 1984; Carr 1986; Carew 1979; Curnock and Hardiker 1979; Hearn 1982; Sibeon 1991a). Nevertheless, there remains no clear answer to the question since diametrically opposed opinions have arisen due to methodological weakness. Suffice to say that, whilst an in-depth answer to the question cannot be provided here, social work students' thirst for critical social theory has already been noted. In addition, the research upon which this chapter is based indicated that CQSW and DipSW qualified social workers used these theories as guides to action.

The characteristic of this social work approach lies in its practical concern with the particular needs of the personal, and its theoretical knowledge base which is constituted from a mesh of psychology and sociology (Payne 1991). In other words, although social work is characterised by its practical focus on the individual, it is also infused with a recognition that, rather than existing in a vacuum, social workers and clients are products of social structure. In contrast to the paternalistic housing officer, who considers his actions to be benevolent, the social worker's sociological understanding of the individual's location within an oppressive social structure might encourage her to adopt an anti-professional approach. Indeed, it is because the social worker recognises that the purpose of her function involves the enforcement of normalcy and social control, that a reflexive approach to assessment encounters is adopted.

> I say to people 'I don't want all this power but I've got it so, you know, so you tell me what you want and I'll get it'. (Social Worker)

> ...you need to think about what you're doing cos you're interfering with people's lives really. I shouldn't say interfering but, erm, well I suppose. But you are in a powerful position really so you should be thinking about what you are doing. (Social Worker)

Nevertheless, despite this recognition, the social worker cannot escape from the fact that her function is based on the relationship between herself and the 'client' (and not herself and social change). This being so, social work discourses that construct personal problems as social creations can only, by implication and necessity, partially extend beyond the rhetorical and infuse practice.

> I'd rather be doing it than someone else because at least I realise what I am doing and can be careful about doing it. (Social Worker)

Reflecting this, the practice of knowledgeable social work can only ever be the result of compromise. This compromise involves creating a picture of the individual that is both personal, in that it presents a subjective view, and social, in that it shows how that person is created and affected by their social surroundings (Payne 1991).

> The only difference I do find with them [social service workers and housing managers] is that they don't have that awareness that I have from the social work course. I mean, I always look at the structure of society and where the person is in it and how they got there. (Social Worker)

> Social work looks at the whole thing, whereas an OT looks at the physical side and housing people tend to look at what pigeon hole they fit into...and a district nurse will look at the medical needs. I think in social work, we...look at it as a whole. (Social Worker)

To do this, the social worker uses her sociological and psychological knowledge to enable her to arrive at a 'situationalised' understanding of the problems that people experience, in a way that enables her to differentiate them from those experienced by others. In doing so, the knowledgeable social worker assesses need, within the particularistic context of the personal situation (i.e. psychological life, e.g. biographical life) and social situation (i.e. sociological life, e.g. housing life). Reflecting this, knowledgeable social work is underpinned by the assumption that, no matter how small or insignificant a problem may appear at the point of referral, the assessment encounter should take place, as far as possible, without prior assumptions being made about the person or their situation.[1]

> I think it's a general assumption [of social work] that you don't know what you're going to meet...I think there's always the assumption that it might not be as clear cut as what you think. (Social Worker)

In order to locate *the problem* within the context of the individual's 'total life', the social work method requires time and a high degree of emphasis on the *personal relationship* between the social worker and the person.

> I mean you're not going to go into a great long question-and-answer routine. Because sometimes you might not always get the full picture on your first visit, you would go back a couple of times...you go in and I suppose its with you actually talking with that person and you ask them if there's anything troubling them at the moment, and it's amazing sometimes how much people want to tell somebody, if they don't have the contact with many people they tell you some very personal information. (Social Worker)

1   Other social work writers (notably Stuart Rees and Gilbert Smith) have criticised social work on the grounds that it is infused with moralism. Whilst I agree with these writers *to a large degree*, my argument is constructed at a different analytical level and thus differs for several reasons. First, it differs by virtue of the comparisons that I am making with housing management. Second, I am using data from interviews with social workers who posessed a CQSW knowledgeability of critical social theory. Other 'social workers', who have been excluded from my analysis, (e.g. unqualified social workers, social work assistants and so on), do adopt moral standpoints because they use 'common sense' (i.e. accepted moral values) as knowledgeable resources, rather than critical theory. Finally, others have looked at social work in a 'case work' context where knowledge has been used for normalising purposes, that is *psychological adjustment*. However, I am concerned with the use of *the same* knowledge, but when it is redeployed within a 'care management' context. Here, knowledge is *instead* used to reveal *psychological need*. In many instances, the application of this knowledge will 'tell' the social worker that there is a *need* to pursue a far from normal solution (as the case of Mary in the text shows). This redeployment of the same stock of knowledge has thus had the empowering consequences that I am describing.

> If I can, I do two visits initially to get to know the person ...So I go and introduce myself and get the initial notes and go back, and usually its a bit more relaxed the second time...It's just a case of teasing it out of people, which can take a couple of visits, assessing what the problem is. Quite often, the problem that you go out and see isn't actually what the problem is. That's what our role is. Trying to tease out what the problem might be. (Social Worker)

This contrasts with the impersonal approach of housing management which, as we have seen, 'objectively identifies' the needs of housing applicants through the use of categories on self-completion assessment forms (perhaps also incorporating a one-off 'visit' into the assessment process for more 'complicated' cases). Conversely, the situationalism that is implicated in knowledgeable social work entails approaching each 'case' as exceptional and unusual, and perforce avoids operating through bureaucratic procedures. This being so, when questioned about the new community care emphasis on form filling rather than 'doing social work', social workers demonstrate a recalcitrance to do as they are told and simply complete assessment forms in the standard fashion required by their managers:

> How do you go to a client in distress and say 'here's the form' and just go through the form? I would never turn up with a form. I have these various topics written down on a pad and then when I went into a client I would, I didn't ever take the pad out first of all. I would talk to them first of all...then say 'is it OK if I take some notes?' and then start with glancing at these topics and taking notes down. (Social Worker)

> ...now we just do community care assessments...but I think if you try to maintain your practice as social work and *bring the assessment into the way we work and not the other way around.* (Social Worker)

Despite the situationalism that this implies, proponents of the 'social model of disability' have suggested that the psychological aspect of the social work function constitutes 'total oppression' (see Oliver 1993; Sapey and Hewitt 1993). This is based on the misplaced notion that social workers only use psychological knowledge for the purpose of *pathological adjustment,* and thus neglect to consider the notion that disablement has a social dimension. However, given that social workers also utilise psychological knowledge in order to understand the wider context within which *personal needs* are situated, it is surely ridiculous to adopt the unquestioning anti social work stance employed by Oliver and his colleagues. It is this psychological understanding of subjective expressions of 'felt' need that perforce necessitate social workers to develop solutions that acknowledge the *ontological need*[2] of older and disabled people to pursue unique and unconventional lifestyles.

Since 'feelings' issues are highly significant (particularly to older people), this is an important point with implications that should be considered further. The social worker's psychological emphasis on the subjective expression of 'felt' need often requires her to go to extreme lengths to maintain older and disabled people in housing situations that, according to a technical or objective understanding of housing need, might be considered intolerable, unhealthy or even a risk to life. On this point, Allen (1997b) provides an extreme example of how one social worker's 'total life' approach to assessment resulted in her acknowledgement that Mary's ontological need to remain in her 'unfit' housing situation should override any concerns that this would involve considerable risk.

> [Mary is] living in a caravan in an awful state really but it's her choice to stay there...She made her nephew swear that she can. The situation that she is living in is extreme...She lives on the floor of the caravan. She is unable to get out of the caravan if there was any fire...To move her would kill her. She's so grateful that she's not being taken away. That's what she always thought would happen. That she would be lifted out of the caravan. If they tried to lift her out of the caravan, she would die going out of the door. Because she is eccentric she was referred as a mental health case. (Social Worker; emphasis added)

This social worker's commitment to the ontological needs of Mary was so great that she was prepared to pursue this extreme course of action in opposition to the wishes of the housing manager and medical practitioners involved with the case (whose objective understandings of her housing and health needs pointed them towards a residential care solution). In doing this, the social worker's orientation and confidence to argue for Mary's *right* to remain in the caravan (against the 'obje-

---

2   In order to arrive at non-reductionist understandings of the individual in society-academics have increasingly engaged in inter-disciplinary theorising. In particular, fusions of sociological and psychological theories have resulted in the development of the concept of 'ontological security' (see Giddens 1984).

ctive' judgements of these others) emanated from her educational grounding in the sociologies of normalcy and deviance:

> 'you've got to be careful that you're not coming in with value judgements.'
> (Social Worker)

Conversely, the approach *suggested* by the BCODP (and some proponents of the 'social model') reduces the needs of older and disabled people to technical (albeit structural) housing need factors that exist outside the person. There is a certain irony in the logical derivative that the insensitivity of this approach to issues about feelings might have otherwise denied Mary's ontological need to remain in the caravan and to pursue her deviant lifestyle.

Conclusion: back to the future for a post modern social work

The aim of this chapter has been to examine whether social workers should be required to involve housing managers in their assessments of housing and community care need. The reason that this constitutes an important issue for contemporary social work practice is linked to the wider post modernist notion that joint work equals good work. This question has been approached by analysing the differing approaches taken by social workers and housing managers to assessing the housing needs of older and disabled people. Table 5.1 provides a summary of the differences of approach that have been presented in the text, and has been adapted from Payne (1991).

The most popular contention that I examined was the notion that the housing problems of community care users should be assessed by housing managers (rather than social workers), given that the former possess an expert knowledge of housing need.

> Is it adequate or appropriate that housing demand is filtered by professional judgements...especially when the professionals concerned are usually professionals from agencies other than housing?...Will [community care users] have to rely in future on needs assessment by care managers, with all this implies about housing being a secondary, rather than a primary concern? (Watson, 1994)

Table 5.1: Social workers, housing managers and the housing needs
of older and disabled people

Feature	Social Work	Housing Management
Individualisation	people are treated as individuals, not categories	people are treated as categories, not individuals
Use of knowledge	personal problems are subjectively understood (through the use of psychological and sociological knowledge) within the context of their situation	tenants and their situation are objectively understood according to technocratic criteria
Relationships with clients	Social work operates through personal relationships	housing management operates through impersonal standardised procedures and routines
Definition of need	need defined through interactive relationship between social worker and client	need defined according to pre-determined criteria

This chapter has shown that it is indeed appropriate for housing need to be assessed by social workers. This is because the issue of importance is not whether assessors possess a technical *knowledge* of housing need. Rather, the salient issue relates to the extent with which the *approach* taken to assessment is able to unearth the unpredictable and contingent housing problems of the personal. Evidently, the technocratic approach of housing managers is entirely inconsistent with the need to unearth subjective expressions of housing need. The social work approach, on the other hand, is based on a method that places the subjective expression of need at the core of the assessment. Despite lacking a 'technical knowledge' of housing need, the extent to which the social work approach incorporates both 'objective' and 'subjective' indicators of housing need is impressive. Indeed, given social work's 'holistic' emphasis on considering the problems of the personal as sociologically and psychologically 'situated', it would be more surprising if the housing situation of clients formed anything less than a central feature of the assessment en-

counter. For Watson (1994) to argue that housing need is a secondary consideration to the social work assessment thus demonstrates a misunderstanding of social
work method. It is spurious for other housing researchers to make the statement
that social workers

> ...remain stubbornly attached to outdated institutional models of care and the
> questionable concept of 'special needs' accommodation...Assessment [is]
> rooted in...diagnostic/pathological dependency categories imposed by prof-
> essional orthodoxy which might lead to adverse stereotyping of the person,
> their needs and possible ways of meeting these needs.
> (Arnold *et al.* 1993, pp.28 and 32)

Clearly, there is now a need for housing researchers to become more cognisant
with the nature of social work knowledge and practice because, at present, the arguments of Arnold, Watson and associates have been constructed from the inaccu-
rate innuendoes and ill-informed anecdotes of housing managers. Indeed, this
chapter has demonstrated that the undesirable characteristics that have been erro-
neously attributed to the social work method are, somewhat ironically, accurate
descriptions of the housing management approach. Paradoxically enough, this
constitutes an important reason that could be invoked by social workers to argue
against those who proclaim that housing managers should assume the central role
in assessing the housing needs of older and disabled people. Indeed, to turn this on
its head, the contention that social workers need to become more cognisant with
housing issues (and, in particular, to conduct 'joint work' with housing managers)
is therefore something of a red herring. Why should social workers be required to
acquire *housing skills,* or even to work with functionaries with *housing skills* when, as
we have seen, these skills contribute little, if anything, to unearthing the subjective
needs that older and disabled people experience or express?

This brings us to the wider question of post modernism, 'joint working' and
knowledgeable competence within which debates about community care have
been located, albeit implicitly and without acknowledgement. We began this
chapter with the observation that post modernism's emphasis on the particularism
and contingency of need has highlighted the need for assessors to adopt a 'holistic'
perspective on personal problems. This was seen perforce to engender an emphasis
on generic training rather than specialist education, and has encouraged the notion
that holistic work necessitates, by implication, 'joint work'. However, herein lies

the paradox. If we take this post modern rhetoric at face value we will be drawn to the same conclusions as those of the housing researchers (myself included) discussed in this chapter. Conversely, if we peer beneath the cultural surface of post modernism, it is apparent that social work education, which has until recently been grounded in an appreciation of sociological and psychological theories, provides the very foundation upon which personal problems can be addressed in highly particular and contingent ways. This is an important point. First, if 'user led' community care is to become a reality, this means reversing the current project of the CCETSW, which aims to strip social work courses of their theoretical content in favour of an emphasis on skills (Howe 1991; Sibeon 1991a, 1991b). Second, as I have already noted, this has opened up the possibility that 'joint work' can also be 'bad work', in particular when housing managers lack the knowledgeable competence to engage in a role that extends beyond the technocratic management of 'bricks and mortar'.

This implies that, if the CIH is serious about social workers engaging in 'joint work' with housing managers, the housing knowledge that it is responsible for validating must be grounded in a general appreciation of the social and psychological theories upon which social work is (or at least, once was) constructed. Broadly speaking, this would mean ensuring that housing managers, like knowledgeable social workers, recognise that everything they do is theoretically subjective (rather than technically objective). To this end, the CIH would need to ensure that housing managers, like knowledgeable social workers, possessed an explicit theoretical (and not just technical) framework within which the consequences of their actions could be reflexively appraised. The paradoxical outcome of such an endeavour would, of course, be that housing managers might be moulded into 'part-time' social workers. Whilst this *could* then enable them to adopt a more reflexive approach to the insular tasks of housing management, there would then seem little point in 'joint work' at all. In other words, no matter which way we approach the issue of joint working, the conclusions that emerge appear to tell us that it is perhaps more appropriate for social workers to 'do social work', for housing managers to (more reflexively) manage bricks and mortar, and for us to forget about joint working altogether! Of course, this is not to say that never the twain should meet. Rather it implies that social workers only need to approach the 'interface' in order to elicit housing resources (e.g. access to what the social worker and their 'client' consider to be an appropriate dwelling) from housing managers who would then, one would hope, respond to such requests in a more reflexive and flexible manner. Chartered Institute for Housing – over to you!

References

Allen, C. (1997a) 'The policy and implementation of the housing role in community care – a constructionist theoretical perspective.' *Housing Studies 12*, 1, 85–110.

Allen, C. (1997b) The significance of 'home' to the structure of disability: a sociological exploration of situated bodies and their emotions. Paper presented at the conference 'Culture and Space in the Home Environment–Critical Evaluations/New Paradigms', Istanbul Technical University, 4th–6th June.

Allen, C., Clapham, D. and Franklin, B. (1995) *The Future of Care in the Community*. Edinburgh: Scottish Homes.

Allen, C. and Gurney, C. (1997) Editorial: 'Beyond housing and social theory.' *European Network for Housing Research 97*, 3, 3–5.

Allen, C. and Walker, R. (1994) *Implementing Community Care*. Cardiff: Welsh Local Government Association.

Arnold, P. (1992) 'Housing and community care: Bricks and mortar or foundation for action?' Paper presented to the Housing Studies Association Conference 'Urban Housing Markets', University of Edinburgh, 21st–22nd September.

Arnold, P., Bochel, H., Brodhurst, S. and Page, D. (1993) *Community Care: The Housing Dimension*. York: Joseph Rowntree Foundation.

Arnold, P. and Page, D. (1992) *Housing and Community Care: Bricks and Mortar or Foundation for Action? A Report to the Major City Council's Housing Group*. Hull: Humberside Polytechnic.

Atkinson, S. (1995) *Cultural Barriers and Community Care Assessments: The Housing Question*. Swansea: Shelter.

Barbour, R.S. (1984) 'Social work education: tackling the theory-practice dilemma.' *British Journal of Social Work 14*, 6, 557–578.

Brennan, W.C. (1973) 'The practitioner as theoretician.' *Journal of Education for Social Work 13*, 1, 5–12.

Carew, R. (1979) 'The place of knowledge in social work activity.' *British Journal of Social Work 9*, 3, 349–364.

Carr, W. (1986) 'Theories of theory and practice.' *Journal of the Philosophy of Education 20*, 2, 177–186.

Chartered Institute of Housing (1996a) *Housing Management Standards Manual – Volume I*. Coventry: Chartered Institute of Housing.

Chartered Institute of Housing (1996b) *Housing Management Standards Manual – Volume II*. Coventry: Chartered Institute of Housing.

Clarke, J. (1996) 'After social work.' In N. Parton (ed) *Social Theory, Social Change and Social Work*. London: Routledge.

Clapham, D. (1994) 'The role of housing in community care.' Paper presented to the 'Housing Policy and Research Priorities' Conference, 22nd–24th March, Glasgow.

Clapham, D. and Franklin, B. (1994a) *The Housing Management Contribution to Community Care.* Glasgow: Centre for Housing Research and Urban Studies.

Clapham, D. and Franklin, B. (1994b) *Housing Management, Community Care and Competitive Tendering.* Coventry: Chartered Institute of Housing.

Curnock, K. and Hardiker, P. (1979) *Towards Practice Theory: Skills and Methods in Social Assessments.* London: Routledge.

Department of the Environment (1997) *Checklist on Housing and Community Care for Discussion with Local Authorities.* Department of the Environment Internet Web Site:http://www.open.gov.uk/doe/houcon/hppa/upchck.htm

Giddens, A. (1984) *The Constitution of Society: Outline of the Theory of Structuration.* Cambridge: Polity Press.

Gurney, C. (1991) 'Millstones and milestones: the experience of home and home ownership.' Paper presented at the British Sociological Association 'Health and Society' conference, University of Manchester, 25th–28th March.

Hallett, C. (1991) 'The children act 1989 and community care: comparisons and contrasts.' *Policy and Politics 19,* 4, 283–291.

Hearn, J. (1982) 'The problems(s) of theory and practice in social work and social work education.' *Issues in Social Work Education 2,* 2, 95–118.

Holmans, A. (nd) *Housing Demand and Need in England 1991–2011.* York: York Publishing Services.

Hopkins, J. (1996) 'Social work through the looking glass.' In N. Parton (ed) *Social Theory, Social Change and Social Work.* London: Routledge.

Howe, D. (1987) *An Introduction to Social Work Theory.* Aldershot: Wildwood House.

Howe, D. (1991) 'The family and the therapist: towards a sociology of social work method.' In M. Davies (ed) *The Sociology of Social Work.* London: Routledge.

Jones, C. (1996) 'Anti-intellectualism and the peculiarities of British social work education.' In N. Parton (ed) *Social Theory, Social Change and Social Work.* London: Routledge.

Joseph Rowntree Foundation (1954) *One Man's Vision: The Story of the Joseph Rowntree Village Trust.* London: Allen and Unwin.

Kemeny, J. (1992) *Housing and Social Theory.* London: Routledge.

Leigh, C. (1994) *Everybody's Baby: Implementing Community Care for Single Homeless People.* London: CHAR.

Macfarlane, A. and Laurie, L. (1996) *Demolishing 'Special Needs': Fundamental Principles of Non-Discriminatory Housing.* Derby: British Council of Organisations of Disabled People.

Malpass, P. And Murie, A. (1990) *Housing Policy and Practice.* London: Macmillan.

Oliver, M. (ed) (1993) *Social Work: Disabled People and Disabling Environments.* London: Jessica Kingsley Publishers.

Parton, N. (ed) (1996) *Social Theory, Social Change and Social Work.* London: Routledge.

Payne, M. (1991) *Modern Social Work Theory: A Critical Introduction.* London: Macmillan.

Payne, M. (1995) *Social Work and Community Care.* London: Macmillan.

Provan, B. and Williams, P. (1991) 'Joining the professionals? the future of housing staff and their work.' In D. Donnison and D. Maclennan (eds) *The Housing Service of the Future.* London: Longman.

Sapey, B. and Hewitt, N. (1993) 'The changing context of social work practice.' In M. Oliver (ed) *Social Work, Disabled People and Disabling Environments.* London: Jessica Kingsley Publishers.

Scottish Homes (1993) *Care in the Community: Policy Statement.* Edinburgh: Scottish Homes.

Scottish Homes (1995) *Care in the Community: Housing Management Procedural Framework.* Edinburgh: Scottish Homes.

Sibeon, R. (1991a) *Towards a New Sociology of Social Work.* Aldershot: Averbury.

Sibeon, R. (1991b) 'The construction of a contemporary sociology of social work.' In M. Davies (ed) *The Sociology of Social Work.* London: Routledge.

Spicker, P. (1993) *Housing and the Social Services.* London: Longman.

Watson, L. (1994) 'Support for a change.' *Housing,* December/January.

Webb, D. (1996) 'Regulation for radicals: the state, CCETSW and the academy.' In N. Parton (ed) *Social Theory, Social Change and Social Work.* London: Routledge.

Welsh Office (1992) *Housing and Community Care,* circular H51–29–19.

Whitehead, C. and Kleinman, M. (1992) *A Review of Housing Needs Assessment.* London: The Housing Corporation.

CHAPTER 6

The Organisation of Social Services and Housing

David Wiseman and Jim Hayton

Social work and housing services are essentially part of the same process, both being concerned with the delivery of services aimed at improving the quality of life for individuals and their families in the community. Consequently, the need to develop an understanding of the nature of the problems they share, and of how resources can jointly be utilised to impact on these problems, should be axiomatic. To the extent that we fail to achieve this, we run the risk of duplication of effort, or–still worse–conflicting approaches to how issues are to be resolved. Both situations will incur an opportunity cost in terms of wasted resources.

If this analysis is accepted, the question for social work and housing professionals becomes one of *how* the process of collaboration is to be initiated and managed thereafter. It is this question that leads us to examine, in this chapter, the potential for joint departments and joint local offices and more generally, how good communication and working together can be achieved, particularly in the light of local government reorganisation. We also briefly examine whether social work and housing managers have a community development role in local area-based strategies.

We have written this chapter as practitioners with a specific experience within Scotland, which has already been outlined above. The main aim of our paper is to draw out practice implications of the previous thinking and research which we have updated through a number of interviews with senior Housing and Social Work managers in Scotland. While practice in Scotland provides the immediate context for much of this chapter, the problems and broad solutions apply throughout the United Kingdom, and also resonate with developments and debates in Europe and further afield.

There has been a lot of research on joint working, particularly in the field of community care, but the emphasis has been on relations between health and social services professions and organisations. Research on the housing–social services interface has mainly focused on the role of housing organisations in community care planning and implementation (see for example Arnold *et al.* 1993; Arnold and Page 1992; and Allen and Walker 1994). The general conclusion seems to be that housing agencies are given only a marginal role in community care planning and are only drawn into other activities (such as needs assessment) when social services staff judge that their input is useful. The overall impression in much of this work is that there are inherent tensions between social workers and housing managers and a mutual lack of understanding based on different methods and styles of working. This was illustrated in the work of Clapham and Franklin (1994) who examined the way that both professions constructed the boundaries between them.

Research on the relationships between housing and social work has rarely focused on the organisational structures of integration. This may reflect academics' concern with organisational processes rather than structures, in the belief that structures are less important and should reflect processes. Nevertheless, this has left practitioners in a vacuum as they are forced to devise organisational structures particularly following local government reorganisation and the creation of unitary authorities. The key issue which has arisen in this process is about the advantages and disadvantages of having a combined housing and social services department. The only research available on this is by Cole (1993) in the early 1990s. Her conclusion was that integration was not well developed between the two professions even in combined departments although there were some interesting examples where a closer integration was attempted with mixed results. The primary motivation to create a unified department was cost saving rather than concern over the quality of the service provided.

This research was a first examination of a very important topic of great contemporary relevance. By itself, though, it provides little guidance to aid thise who have the job of devising working organisations. Therefore we are forced to rely almost exclusively on the experience of those working in the field in the light of the dearth of more systematic evidence.

Has local government reorganisation removed the primary organisational obstacle to joint working?

Until the creation of the new unitary local authorities, many commentators saw the division of functions of social work and housing (in Scotland, between District and Regional Councils, and in England and Wales between Non-Metropolitan Counties and District Councils) as the most obvious obstacle to the development of good joint working.

This division was highlighted in the 1960s by the Seebohm Committee (1968) and the Royal Commission on Local Government in Scotland (1969). The Seebohm Committee concluded 'We have arrived at the firm conclusion that a family service cannot be fully effective until the social services department and the housing, education and health departments are the undivided responsibility of the same local authority' (HMSO 1968). The Royal Commission stated that 'the Seebohm Committee has shown in the most authoritative way how close the relationships are between...the personal social services and housing. We agree wholeheartedly...that one authority should administer them all' (HMSO 1969).

Thirty years later the establishment of unitary authorities has now removed this obstacle. It will be interesting to see with the benefit of hindsight whether the existence of separate authorities represented a somewhat spurious excuse for not creating greater collaboration at an earlier date and whether local government reorganisation will now lead to new ways of joint working between the two services to the mutual benefit of service users. It is still too early to be able to answer this question, and so we turn instead to the issue of how the process of collaboration is to be initiated and managed in the light of these recent changes.

To examine this latter question we interviewed a number of senior managers within four of the newly established Scottish unitary authorities (Stirling, Clackmannanshire, West Dumbarton and West Lothian) that have either already established joint social work and housing departments or were preparing to establish a joint department. In Scotland, while most of the new unitary authorities have retained traditional models, about 25 per cent have opted for joint housing and social work departments. We also reviewed some of the literature already published on the question of integration of social work and housing and considered our own experience of collaboration and joint working in a unitary authority which has retained separate social work and housing departments.

The framework we used for our interviews was based on the key questions out-lined in the research report *Just Good Friends?* (Cole 1993), and consequently the main strands of our analysis are the advantages and disadvantages of a unified housing and social services department, any significant changes engendered by in-tegration, and other general issues.

Our conclusion is that a joint department is *not* a prerequisite to good practice in joint working. In the main, this was also the view of those we interviewed, who felt that any benefits gained were not really advantages which arose from joint de-partments *per se* but were those which could and would arise from collaborative practice and joint working under existing organisational arrangements.

It is our view therefore that the primary question should be what *form* of joint arrangements will result in effective, efficient, good quality social work and hous-ing services being provided. In some cases, because of local circumstances, the con-clusion is that the way forward is to have an integrated social work and housing service, but in others that they should remain as separate services working effec-tively together. From this perspective, the issue is much more about the develop-ment of good horizontal links between the services. There is no certainty that joint departments will function more effectively than separate departments. Different models will be appropriate for different situations.

In the remainder of the chapter we explain the grounds for the above conclu-sion and suggest how effective collaboration and joint working can be initiated and managed, either within joint departments or between two separate services.

Joint working

Joint working involves joint planning, accountability, financial control, location and access, communication, efficiency and effectiveness, and training and devel-opment. We will consider each of these, before summarising the advantages and disadvantages of joint departments.

Joint planning

Social Services and Housing currently have different requirements in terms of the production of statutory plans. The key document in the case of housing is the Housing Plan, whereas the Community Care and Children's Services Plans fulfil this function for the Social Services. In Scotland a Criminal Justice Services Plan is also required. Despite the difference in content and emphasis, some of those interviewed believed that the biggest advantage of all was in the area of joint planning. Previous research (Clapham and Franklin 1994) indicated that at senior management level, relations between social services and housing departments had improved, aiding the joint planning process. However, the researchers also suggested that housing managers were still unclear of their role and felt relegated to a peripheral position. In the interviews we carried out it was suggested that, in joint departments, planning was more comprehensive in that while there were still separate service plans, it was likely that these were more clearly linked through a service statement which affirmed common goals. In one of the authorities the same group of people produce all of the statutory plans pertaining to the joint department (i.e. the team writing the Housing Plan also prepares the Community Care Plan) leading to awareness of respective policies, resources, constraints and so on. This innovative approach of having one team jointly prepare all plans merits further investigation, although similar co-operation might be ach- ieved through a joint planning team or alternative arrangement without necessarily having to have a joint department.

The main planning advantages of a joint department were seen as the potential for developing:

- joint understanding of the comprehensive needs of communities – both housing investment needs, and the specific care needs of individuals
- a good foundation of shared data (confidentiality permitting, data should be shared and stored in a common format)
- links between various statutory plans and land use plans (local and structure plans) could have direct benefits, for example, in discharging social work's criminal justice responsibility, in Scotland, through rehousing ex-offenders
- a process that ensures that the revenue component of a care project is not overlooked or underestimated at the planning stage.

A particular benefit perceived by one senior manager was the potential for the priority needs of social work clients to receive a higher profile, for example, when housing investment and regeneration schemes were being developed. The same manager also felt that the huge changes that had already taken place in the culture of local authority housing departments over the past ten years, resulting to a large extent from the move away from direct provision to an enabling role, could bring direct benefits to a joint department. In particular, by bringing to the joint department housing-based entrepreneurial skills which were not yet as widely developed in social work departments, where a traditional client-centred approach still prevails. On the other hand, she felt that social work had better developed planning processes and was good at 'owning' the planning process and involving operational staff as part of the process. Therefore, housing might also benefit from the partnership. In any event it was suggested that the Joint Community Care Plan, the Housing Plan and Housing Management Plan all required cross-service representation on planning groups.

Accountability

One of the potential disadvantages perceived as arising from a joint department was the possibility that accountability could become blurred. This was one of the early concerns raised by the Association of Directors of Social Work (ADSW) who felt that there was a need to identify precisely how the newly established joint departments ensured a clear focus on accountability. A particular concern was that the person with ultimate responsibility for social work services (the qualified chief social work officer, required by law in Scotland) should also have control over resources. It was felt that the test would be in the chief social work officer's direct access to elected members, (access which Scottish Office guidance expects), in the context of a joint department headed by someone other than the chief social work officer.

Financial control

The statutory requirement for a separate Housing Revenue Account was seen by at least one of the senior managers interviewed as an unambiguous benefit for service delivery. This meant that he did not have to rely on annual government grant and could control his own rent charge levels. He also felt that this allowed his service to internalise many of the commercial disciplines of business practice. The possibility also then emerges of increasing expenditure elsewhere on new initiatives through efficiency savings. Therefore, there was a great incentive for strong financial control and none of the annual competition with other services for financial resources, or redistribution of funding at the will of the Chief Executives or the Council to other political priorities.

However, where joint initiatives with social work are under discussion the possibility of mixing two funding sources in imaginative and flexible ways opens up a number of interesting options. One example given was where the Housing side of a joint service had decided to recruit its own Occupational Therapist to tackle adaptations for disabled people and similar issues, as well as to provide additional back-up to colleagues in the social work side of the joint department.

From her experience, one of the senior managers believed that housing managers brought a greater financial acumen, through their experience of managing devolved local budgets, and thereby were better able to prioritise and contain expenditure. She also felt that the information technology required to facilitate this kind of management accountability was more prevalent in housing. In her opinion social work needed to develop more effective systems for performance monitoring (including generating their own performance indicators rather than relying on those required by the Accounts Commission). She recognised however that social work performance measures in areas of child care may be more complex than measuring performance in most aspects of the housing service.

Location and customer access

The author of *Just Good Friends* (Cole 1993) suggested that a common theme running through discussions with senior officers and staff concerned the advantages to be gained from situating housing and social work staff in the same geographical location, sharing offices at points of service access and delivery.

However, given that, particularly in respect of social work services, not all of the specialist services provided will be located within each and every local office, overlapping customers requiring both services will often have to visit more than one location. For most customers this is not an issue because the vast majority of housing customers do not require any social work input. Indeed some might resent the potential stigma of carrying out their housing business in what was an integrated housing/social work office environment.

The fact that not all specialist services can be available in each location, and the perception of stigma, cannot be used as excuses for making our customers jump through a number of hoops before being able to present their enquiry or problem. Our own preference is for a combination of corporate 'one–door/one stop' shops (providing access to the majority of local authority services), common office prem-

ises for housing/social work and, where appropriate, separate premises for specialist services.

Communication

Arblaster *et al.* (1996) found that communication between agencies was generally
poor and that there were difficulties in sharing information, particularly confidential information, as well as cultural and professional differences between agencies,
all of which became barriers to effective collaboration. This study identified several issues for consideration:

- communication needs to be developed at all levels of operation both within
  each agency and between agencies
- agencies need to find ways to improve face-to-face and written
  communication
- procedures and practices should be integrated
- methods of sharing confidential and non-confidential information, resolving
  disputes and monitoring needs should be developed.

The majority of the senior managers interviewed felt that the establishment of
joint departments had, or in time would, create improved communications between the two services. Most managers also believed that this would lead to a better mutual understanding of the traditionally quite different cultures and agendas
the two services possessed (or were perceived to have). In other words housing is
often viewed as being concerned with 'bricks and mortar' and group provision,
whereas social work may be preoccupied with care needs and the individual.
Moreover these perspectives are frequently seen as being at odds with each other,
with housing staff seen as being involved in business-type processes where speed
and efficiency are valued, and social work being traditionally more deliberative
and interested in detail and uniqueness of circumstances.

While joint services would not dramatically shift these perspectives, the managers we interviewed were certain that they had the potential to facilitate mutual understanding of each other's approach, and to engender a respect for what
colleagues were trying to achieve, so that co-operation could develop where objectives were mutual and consistent. Similarly, in communication with other local
authority services, elected members and external agencies, staff of a joint depart-

ment could be encouraged to represent both disciplines wherever possible, thereby assisting in the development of corporate identity and reducing wasteful use of scarce staff resources.

Problem resolution: Efficiency and effectiveness

Few would disagree that issues should be resolved at the lowest competent level of the two professions within a joint department (or across the two services where there are separate departments), and whenever possible by consensus. Staff should naturally be encouraged to develop productive local working relationships with colleagues in the companion profession or service.

The managers we interviewed suggested that in a joint department there was an increased awareness of the nature of each other's service, and consequently staff were more willing to address and resolve problems at an earlier stage and within a local context, rather than feeding problems up the ladder to be resolved by senior managers. In three of the four authorities the integration of the two services had taken place at the time of establishing the new unitary authorities and therefore had been part of a review of all of the services that would be the responsibility of the new unitary authority. In the fourth authority the decision had been taken some nine months in to the first year of the new authority and had been taken during the annual budgetary process.

Some interviewees contended not only that the integration of the two services enabled a broader strategic view of the two services but also thought the arrangement could eliminate duplication of effort through the greater opportunity for joint working. The potential for joint offices and sharing of support staff (e.g. personnel, administrative, financial) was also mentioned as leading to greater efficiency, although in most cases it was too early for any of these changes to have taken place.

Training and joint development

For obvious reasons of core professional specialisation there will be detailed aspects of both social work and housing training which will have limited significance for the other service. There is still a pressing need however for mutual understanding of the culture of each service if constructive relationships are to be developed. Issues such as rent arrears control, coping with anti-social or criminal behaviour, community care needs, the implementation of childrens legislation and homelessness advice and assistance, are all points of significant contact between social work and housing services.

Clapham and Franklin (1994) refer to there often being resentment and hostility between front line housing and social services workers, largely due to a lack of mutual understanding about tasks and priorities.

Arblaster *et al.* (1996) considered the extent to which agencies work together to address the needs of those living in ordinary housing, the barriers to effective collaboration and how these might be overcome. From a series of interviews they found that housing, health and social care agencies were not effectively collaborating to provide services for vulnerable people living in ordinary houses. They stated that links between social services and health were reasonably good, but that both tended to exclude housing. They also found that there was a widespread lack of understanding of the roles and responsibilities of other agencies and about the boundaries between them.

The need for greater understanding of the roles, responsibilities and constraints of the different services was confirmed in our interviews with senior managers, as well as from our own experience. Therefore it is our view that a fundamental need exists for joint induction training to be provided to all social work and housing workers. This training should cover, in the first instance, the respective (statutory) responsibilities of each service and the full range of services offered by each. It should also focus on particular (and historical) areas of contention such as evictions and the respective statutory, professional and ideological views which govern the approach of the different services to issues such as these.

Basic training should also cover the constraints on each service, especially resource constraints. There should be a module covering how the relevant budgets of each service are formulated, distributed and managed. There must be a corporate element to the training (i.e. consideration of the local authority's objectives as opposed to professional or departmental agendas) and, since we live in the real world, a political perspective at a senior level is imperative. Key outputs of the training sessions—and key factors in joint development—should include agreement on the ways in which a shared 'modus operandi' will be developed and on the principle of developing some kind of service level statement of shared values and a basic procedure for resolving issues as they arise.

As part of the continuing dialogue to emerge from joint training, factors such as the extent and consequences of co-location need to be addressed. Indeed the range of solutions which might be appropriate needs to be examined. These could vary from joint offices to the placement or secondment of staff within the respective offices of each service. We feel strongly that only when officers in the respective professions fully understand the services they each provide, and the issues facing them in doing so, can each identify their potential contribution to the other at the interface, thereby improving service delivery. With many local authorities seeking to achieve a one-door approach to services, joint training can bring economies of scale, dispel professional mystique, lead to and aid understanding of the respective roles of different staff within the local authority, and thereby help towards the provision of more efficient and effective services which should provide greater value for money.

What has changed in the joint departments?

It must again be stressed that local government reorganisation, and the formation of joint departments, is still in a formative stage, and the following comments must be viewed in that context.

In most cases, although the two services have been brought together in one department, there has been little formal merging of the services below the level of senior management. In the majority of cases Housing and Social Work remain as separate entities. There is a clear desire not to lose the focus that both services need to develop if the variety of problems facing individuals and local communities is to be properly addressed. Some joint housing/social work offices have been opened although in the one authority where this was the case it was stated that future development of joint offices would happen more as a development of a 'one-stop shop' approach to services (and therefore would affect all services not just housing and social work).

Some disadvantages of joint departments

Some concerns were expressed about the perceived loss of status of whichever profession did *not* provide the Chief Officer of the joint department. This could relate to a degree of professional jealousy but also reflected concerns that the lack of understanding of the specialism of either Housing or Social Work might lead to an inability to provide the necessary management and professional support to the 'other' profession.

While in some quarters there is a view that housing and social work should be brought closer together, others would argue that *health* and social work are more likely to be the primary joint partners of the future, particularly if health services are brought into a framework where there is much greater democratic control at a local level.

It is true that housing and social work share a number of factors such as the development of provider and purchaser roles, an enabling role to facilitate a mixed economy, performance management and quality assurance, tenant participation in respect of housing services and user and carer participation in respect of social work services. However, the move towards a more specialist structure within some social work authorities (as against the generic housing management role), and the specific public protection role of some aspects of social work services (child protection, regulation and inspection and, in Scotland, criminal justice services) leads us to question whether the integration of the two services into one department is as attractive as it may appear at first sight.

If it is accepted that all that structures provide is a framework and that what achieves results is the quality, competence, enthusiasm and commitment of individuals working in effective teams, then the important task is to ensure that structures facilitate this effective team working. A paper by Martin (1997) presented to the 1997 Association of Directors of Social Work annual conference makes this case and suggests that traditional structures are designed to meet the needs of the providers, not the consumers of services. Instead, he argues, structures should be built on the needs of local communities and reflect local priorities, because

> the issues facing individuals and communities do not fall into neat boxes that conform to our traditional structures. Issues relate to poverty, unemployment, crime and vandalism, alienation and isolation, environmental pollution, transport and infrastructure, economic development, poor health and housing, and many of these issues overlap and impact on one another. (Martin 1997)

Can social work and housing managers have a community development role in local area-based strategies?

This is a general issue relevant throughout the UK, although in the main we have concentrated on reviewing our own experience within Scotland. However, there is no special reason to believe that this issue is any different in form in Scotland, England, Wales or Northern Ireland.

Before exploring this question we should define what we mean by community development. The definition we use in this instance is one used by the Association of Metropolitan Authorities (AMA 1989). In this publication it was contended that community development is now increasingly accepted as a central strategy for local authorities and other agencies, and is about the involvement of people in the issues which affect their lives. It is a process based on the development of a partnership between all those involved to enable a sharing of skills, knowledge and experience.

Community development can be applied to many different services and activities and is most effective as a strategic approach within a local authority to service planning and delivery. Community development can be defined as the process by which a local authority deliberately stimulates and encourages groups of people to express their needs, supports them in collective action, helps with their projects and schemes, and develops solutions with them to tackling these identified needs.

The AMA publication identified three principles central to community development:

1.   It is based on the importance and the ability of people to act together to influence and assert control over social, economic and political issues which affect them. In this sense community development focuses on the relation between people and the range of institutions and decision makers (public and private) which govern their everyday experiences. Community development aims to effect a sharing of power and create structures which give genuine participation and involvement.

2.   Community development is about involving the skills, knowledge and experience of people in taking initiatives to respond to social, economic and political problems. This will usually involve co-operation or negotiation with statutory agencies at some level.

3.   Community development must take a lead in confronting the attitudes of
     individuals, and the practices of institutions which discriminate against
     black people, women, and other disadvantaged groups. Community
     development is well placed to involve people in these issues which affect
     all of us. (AMA 1989)

In many ways the above principles were a normal part of local authority practice
prior to local government re-organisation. It is too early to say whether that will
change in the light of reorganisation. Already there are some concerns that the
rhetoric of community empowerment and community development is not always
backed up with the resources and support necessary for local community organisations to play a meaningful role in influencing local government decision-making.

Local communities in Scotland have for a long time had a tradition of organising and voicing concerns, trying to influence public policy and the way services are
delivered. Sometimes this type of activity can be uncomfortable for local authorities but some have realised that community organisations have an important role in
enabling services to become more relevant to needs as well as being more cost effective (Hashagan 1995).

Strathclyde Regional Council, in particular, was at the forefront of local government's application of community development principles, in trying to change the
perception of local government from being paternalistic to participatory. Strathclyde's community development strategy sought to recognise the value of seeking
to involve people in defining and developing responses to their own problems
rather than imposing 'expert' solutions. The Council believed that this approach
had the potential to unlock a reservoir of talent and ideas affording the potential
for Strathclyde to plan better and more relevant services in response to the different
needs of local communities.

Although the previous Regional and District Councils shared a commitment to
community development, they often adopted different (and sometimes conflicting) approaches in response to different objectives. The new unitary authorities are
experiencing some tension arising from having brought the two different approaches together.

The Regional Councils adopted broadly based social strategies in which community development was an underlying principle. However, District Councils

tended to focus activity on participation and consultation in relation to housing, which was seen as the most significant service they were responsible for.

The positive achievements of community development in Scottish local authorities in recent years were identified in a recent report on a national consultation carried out in the period prior to Scottish local government reorganisation (Hashagan 1995). This report included the following findings which are relevant to the question being considered:

1. Local authorities were becoming more skilled in working with communities in areas such as assessing community needs, improved practices for consultation, and so on.

2. Local authority officers were prepared to be more accountable to people they work with and for.

3. Local authorities were encouraging more workers to undertake training related to community development.

4. Senior managers were increasingly recognising the relevance of community development values and practices.

5. Some Councils were now prepared to fund local initiatives, allowing recipients to get on with their own development activity.

6. There was a growth in partnership activity involving the local authority, other agencies and local communities.

Writing in 1996, Goodlad reported that:

> In 1993 half of Scotland's housing authorities had a written policy on tenant participation, and half held regular discussion meetings with tenants. Around one-third employed specialist staff such as tenant liaison officers, some of whom have a background in community work, to assist the development of participation. (Goodlad 1996)

This paper went on to state that 'tenant participation in housing management has been largely restricted to a few issues' and later concluded that

> In summary, it should be apparent that community participation has been limited to certain issues and some landlords, and that only in relatively isolated cases has it extended beyond information provision and consultation to negotiation and limited control. (Goodlad 1996)

It is in this somewhat pessimistic context that the question can be posed as to whether social workers and housing managers can have a purposive community development role in local area based strategies.

If it is accepted that some of the outcomes of good community development practice are strong communities leading to more efficient and effective local government which can deliver relevant services in response to different local needs, then the question might be posed in terms of what may be lost if we do not encourage the adoption of a community development perspective for housing and social work professionals. It could be argued from this perspective that we cannot afford *not* to tap the potential reservoir of talent and ideas that exists in most of the communities we serve as local government officers.

Housing managers need to know which groups and organisations exist in any one neighbourhood. They must develop the ability to analyse community needs and resources so that decisions made, not just in respect of housing but in the wider context of their role within local government as a member of a corporate organisation, are based on an understanding of community strengths and networks.

Despite what has been said about the limited role of community participation in housing management there are clear signs that community development approaches have already helped to change the face of housing over a long period of time, with the dramatic growth in the number of community-based housing associations and tenant co-operatives throughout Scotland (and Glasgow in particular) being evidence of the perceived benefits of greater tenant control.

In other fields too local communities have effectively tackled problems when they were given encouragement, support and a means of influencing decisions taken by local authorities (and other agencies) which affect their quality of life; they have come to understand the particular issues and how they may be tackled. The combination of the knowledge and skills of local residents, professionals and others, where this leads to collaborative working, results in the potential for more effective responses to community needs.

Conclusion

As previously stated, our conclusion regarding the question of joint working and joint departments, having carried out the interviews and reviewed the literature, is that a joint department is *not* a prerequisite to good practice in joint working. In the main, this was also the view of those we interviewed, who felt that any benefits gained were not really advantages which arose from joint departments *per se* but were those which could and would arise from collaborative practice and joint working under existing organisational arrangements.

The important point is that we need to establish joint arrangements which result in effective, efficient, good quality social work and housing services being provided. In some cases, because of local circumstances, the way forward will be to have an integrated social work and housing service, but in others the two services should remain as separate services working effectively together. From this perspective, the issue is much more about the development of good horizontal links between the services. There is no certainty that joint departments will function more effectively than separate departments. Different models will be appropriate for different situations.

As regards the second question, 'Can social work and housing managers have a community development role in local area-based strategies?', our conclusion is that, despite the tensions and potential conflict that might arise, they can. In fact we would suggest that they not only can but must do so if we are going to tap the potential reservoir of talent and ideas that exists in most of the communities we serve as local government officers.

References

Allen, C. and Walker, R. (1994) *Implementing Community Care.* Cardiff: Welsh Local Government Association.

AMA (1989) *Community Development – The Local Authority Role.* London: Association of Metropolitan Authorities (AMA).

Arblaster, L., Conway, J., Foreman, A. and Hawtin, M. (1996) *Asking the Impossible? Inter-agency Working to Address the Housing, Health and Social Care Needs of People in Ordinary Housing.* Bristol: Polity Press.

Arnold, P. and Page, D. (1992) *Housing and Community Care: Bricks and Mortar or Foundation for Action? A Report to the Major City Council's Housing Group.* Hull: Humberside Polytechnic.

Arnold, P., Bochel, H., Brodhurst, S. and Page, D. (1993) *Community Care: the Housing Dimension.* York: Joseph Rowntree Foundation.

Clapham, D. and Franklin, B. (1994) *Housing Management, Community Care and Competitive Tendering: A Good Practice Guide.* London: Chartered Institute of Housing.

Cole, M. (1993) *Just Good Friends?* London: Local Government Management Board.

Goodlad, R. (1996) 'Housing policy change and the dilemmas of community participation.' *The Scottish Journal of Community Work and Development 1,* Autumn 1996, 17–32.

Hashagan, S. (1995) *Community Development in Scotland's Unitary Authorities.* Scottish Community Development Centre.

HMSO (1968) *The Seebohm Committee: Committee on Local Authority and Allied Personal Social Services.* Cmnd 3703. London: HMSO.

HMSO (1969) *The Royal Commission on Local Government in Scotland.* Cmnd 4150. London: HMSO.

Martin (1997) Unpublished paper presented to the Association of Directors of Social Work Annual Conference, Aviemore, Scotland.

CHAPTER 7

Women and Housing

Fran Wasoff

Gender is an important dimension for understanding how access to housing is structured, how economic disadvantage translates to housing disadvantage, and how housing disadvantage reinforces economic dependency. It is not only access to housing that is gendered. There are other ways in which housing systems are gendered: in the use and design of housing, in the importance of security and safety in housing design (Woods 1994), and in the meaning of a home (Munro and Madigan 1993). In this chapter the focus will be on issues of housing access and housing disadvantage.

Social work practice which fails to recognise the centrality of housing for women who are users of personal social services will at best be only partly effective and will at worst reinforce the structural disadvantages found by women.

We shall consider women's experience of securing and maintaining access to housing, and how this experience differs from men's. Men and women use housing in different ways (Morris and Winn 1990). This is because of the sexual division of labour in the home, the physical separation of home and work, and travel to work issues, and the design of houses and cities. The chapter will review the evidence that access to housing is gendered.

Access to housing is not only gendered, but varies amongst women according to other structural divisions in society, such as a woman's age, marital status, sexual orientation, social class, past and present labour market activity and whether or not her household includes children. Thus this chapter will also consider how women's access to housing is influenced by other social divisions.

Access to housing is not the single event of getting somewhere to live, but is a continuous process of sustaining access and avoiding losing a home. Some of the difficulties women face in securing and maintaining access to housing reflect and reinforce wider gender inequalities in society. However, the picture is complex since some of the mechanisms for allocating housing reduce the extent of women's structural disadvantage in society.

In recent years, housing has not been prominent on the political agenda. Nevertheless, the previous governments's agenda for rolling back the state produced housing policies that made the distribution of housing by market mechanisms more common, and allocation according to need less frequent. These have combined to make women's access to decent quality housing more difficult.

Women and housing tenure

Most women live in households with other adults, mainly men, and, in many ways, their experience of access to housing will be shared by their households. However, an increasing proportion of women live in female-headed households either on their own or with their children. A small but increasing number of women-headed families share a household with another family.

Thus, at any given time, only a minority of women will live in women-headed households. However, the circumstances of women-headed households are relevant to *all* women, not only those who currently live on their own or with their children. Since a high proportion of women will, at some point in their lives, live in a female-headed household (Morris and Winn 1990), either because they are young and single, separated or divorced, or elderly and living on their own. Moreover, the circumstances of women-headed households can tell us something about all women's opportunities for *independent* access to housing, that is not dependent on having men in their households.

One way of examining differences in access to housing is by looking at the relationship of housing tenure to gender and marital status. Table 7.1, based on evidence from the 1995 General Household Survey, shows that male-headed households are much more likely to be owner occupiers than female-headed households. Nearly three quarters (74%) of all households headed by men are owner occupied, and half of households headed by men are owner occupied with mortgages. Marriage increases the likelihood of home ownership for men; nearly four out of five households (79%) headed by married men are owner occupied. Since the General Household Survey usually classifies the husband as head of

Table 7.1: Housing tenure by sex and marital status of head of household

Heads of household										
	Males					Females				Total
Tenure	Married	Single	Widowed	Divorced/ separated	All males	Single	Widowed	Divorced/ separated	All females	
Owner occupied, owned outright	25	14	50	9	24	15	51	13	30	25
Owner occupied, with mortgage	54	37	10	37	50	27	6	38	21	42
Rented from local authority	12	20	30	28	14	29	30	31	30	18

Source: Living in Britain (1997) The General Household Survey 1995, Table 3.10, p.33.

household in households with married couples, we can infer that a similarly high proportion of married women also live in owner occupied housing, primarily in owner occupied housing with a mortgage. However, owner occupation is much less likely for female-headed households of all types (and for male-headed households of other types). Only about half of female-headed households, that is, women who are single, divorced, separated or widowed, are owner occupiers. Female-headed households are far less likely than male-headed households to be buying their own homes; only one in five female-headed households (21%), compared with half (50%) of male-headed households were owner occupied with mortgages. Female-headed households were more than twice as likely to be renting from a local authority (30%) than male-headed households (14%). Thus, housing policies that have affected the quality and quantity of local authority housing will have a disproportionate impact on female-headed households. Opportunities to become a tenant have decreased substantially, with tenants declining from nearly half (48%) of all households in 1979 to one-third (33%) of households in 1995. As the local authority rented housing sector has shrunk from 34 per cent of all households in 1979 to 18 per cent of all households in 1995 (a reduction only partially compensated for by the growth in housing associations from 1 per cent to 4 per cent of households over the same period, Living in Britain 1997, Table 3.1,

Table 7.2: Tenure of housing in which women live by marital status 1993/94

Great Britain	Married %	Single %	Widow-ed %	Div./sep %	All wo-men %
Owner occupied, owned outright	24	19	50	12	26
Owner occupied, with mortgage	54	39	9	37	44
Rented from local authority/new town	15	24	31	37	20
Rented from housing associa-tion/cooperative	2	5	4	5	3
Rented privately, unfurnished	3	5	6	6	4
Rented privately, furnished	2	8		2	2
Rented with job or business	2	1		1	1
All tenures	100	100	100	100	100

p.29) opportunities to gain access to social rented housing have declined, as have the housing opportunities of those dependent on social rented housing.

Recent data from another source (see Table 7.2) supports the pattern described above. Seventy per cent of women in Britain lived in owner occupied housing in 1993/94, with married women most likely to be in owner occupied housing. Housing tenure is also associated with age. Young women under 25 are most likely to be in private rented housing; women aged 25 to 54 are most likely to live in owner occupied housing with a mortgage and older women and widowed women are most likely to live in owner occupied housing that is owned outright (CSO1995).

Each of the housing tenures have their own means of securing and maintaining access to housing, and each present particular issues for women.

Women-headed households and council housing

Since data on housing tends to be reported in relation to families or households, it is difficult to obtain information about women's access to council housing. However, it is clear that women-*headed* households are particularly reliant on council housing, and form a disproportionately large group of tenants in this sector. These households are headed mainly by lone mothers (see Table 7.1) who are single, divorced or separated, and older women. Despite the local authority sector housing only 18 per cent of all households (ONS 1997, p.29), it accounts for 30 per cent of all female-headed households (Table 7.1). In a 1991 survey quoted by Woods (1996, p.67), of households renting from local authorities in England, 18 per cent were single parents, and 24 per cent were one person female households. A similar pattern applies to housing associations. Thus over 40 per cent of social rented housing is occupied by female-headed households—a much higher proportion than found in the population generally. The higher concentration of female-headed households in council housing is due in part to local authority policies that allocate housing on the basis of need, and women-headed households tend to be amongst those in greatest housing need. But it also reflects the difficulties faced by women on their own in trying to secure and sustain access to housing elsewhere (either owner occupied or private rented housing) so that they have fewer alternatives to social rented housing.

The key changes in housing policy since 1979 include the Housing Acts 1980 and 1988, the Housing (Scotland) Acts 1980 and 1988 and the Local Government and Housing Act 1989. All of these have reduced collective provision of housing to meet housing need. Women-headed households are disproportionately reliant on council housing, so that these changes have had a greater impact on such households. Women council tenants have also been less able to buy their council houses and take advantage of the 1980 Act.

Council housing is distributed according to allocation policies, which are bureaucratic rules based on criteria of need. Since allocation is based on need, rather than the ability to pay, council tenants typically have access to housing that is better than the housing they could otherwise command in the private housing market (owner occupied or private rented). Thus it can be argued that council housing provision is progressive inasmuch as it is provision 'in kind' and part of a 'social wage' package that makes the income of low-income households stretch further. This social wage will disproportionately benefit women-headed households, since these are some of the poorest even in the local authority housing sector. A study carried out by Sefton (1997) measured the extent to which the 'social wage' embodied in social rented housing (and other benefits in kind) reduced the growth of income inequality. Of all the benefits in kind studied, subsidised social rented housing was the most 'pro-poor': it had the greatest impact on redistribution of income in favour of the poor, and thus on low-income female-headed households.

However, council housing is not without its problems for women, and these relate to the availability, cost and quality of council housing.

Availability

One of the most striking changes in the British housing market during the period of Conservative government from 1979 to 1997 has been the marked reduction in the supply of council housing. Due to policies mentioned earlier, the number of council houses has almost halved. Since women-headed households have been particularly dependent on public rented housing, their housing opportunities have diminished, increasing the risk of homelessness and hidden homelessness and forcing women into substandard private rented housing or insecure home ownership.

Cost

There is a serious question as to the affordability of council housing. With the sharp withdrawal of central government housing subsidies to local authorities, council house rents have risen sharply, much more rapidly than inflation or incomes. Combined with other policies, such as the right to buy, this has the effect that a very high proportion of council tenants are dependent on housing benefit, and women-headed households are even more likely to be in receipt of housing benefit. Dependence on housing benefit creates a serious poverty trap, particularly where children are involved, in which women are unable to increase their incomes through employment, since for each pound earned, there is almost a pound in housing benefit lost, leaving women hardly better off.

Quality

With strict government limits on local authority capital expenditure on housing for the last 20 years, there has now been a long period of under-investment in public rented housing. This has meant that very little new council housing has been built, and there is still a substantial backlog of disrepair in the existing housing stock. The spending squeeze, combined with right to buy policies that have removed the most desirable types of property from local authority ownership, has left a disproportionate amount of housing unsuitable for young children, such as in high rise blocks of flats, or housing schemes with serious security problems. Woods (1996) presents evidence that women-headed households are more likely to be housed in the less desirable social rented housing stock in terms of location and quality: in areas with a higher rating on deprivation indices, run-down estates, high rise flats, and so on. While women-headed households in housing need may get access to council housing, the quality, location and security of that housing may leave a great deal to be desired. What's more, the greater a woman's housing need, the more likely it is that she will have no alternative but to accept poor quality housing in a disadvantaged and dangerous area, since she cannot afford to wait for a better offer. Thus, within the public rented sector, allocation policies can add to a household's relative disadvantage, and since women-headed households are amongst the most disadvantaged, they often end up in the poorest quality housing, unsuitable for children.

Many women who come into contact with social workers will face extreme examples of these problems in trying to secure a suitable home for themselves and their families in the social rented sector.

Women and home ownership

Most women are housed in owner occupied housing, primarily as married women living with their husbands. This pattern is consistent with the orientation of government housing policies in favour of the traditional nuclear family.

> The Government's aim is that a decent home should be within the reach of every family...Establishing a home – particularly as a place in which to raise a family – is a matter for which married couples want to feel personally responsible. (DoE 1994, quoted in Pascall 1997, p.33)

Indeed, as Table 7.3 shows, owner occupation is *the* housing tenure for couples; 61 per cent of mortgages are jointly held by one man and one woman. Housing policies give highest priority to housing for married couples with children, thus linking the adequacy of housing for women to their marital status and their position as mothers. So, while women's access to home ownership is most likely to be achieved if they are married, and is therefore associated with their economic dependency on their husbands, women's contribution to mortgage payments probably increases the likelihood that men can secure and sustain home ownership as well. Thus men and women increase each others' chances of securing access to home ownership.

Access to home ownership favours those in well-paid and secure, uninterrupted employment, particularly two-earner households, since home ownership depends on the ability to pay a mortgage over a long period. Thus home ownership is geared more to the typical male employment pattern than to women's employment. Women's independent access to home ownership is constrained by structural disadvantage in the labour market and responsibilities for the care of children and dependent adult relatives. The general patterns of women's employment are familiar enough: women's hourly rates of pay and total income from employment are still significantly lower than men's, women are more likely to work part-time and experience breaks in employment because of family caring responsibilities. Each of these patterns presents difficulties for women who may wish to become home

Table 7.3: Mortgages by gender of borrower

Great Britain	Percentage	
	1983	1994
Women only	8.2	17.2
Men only	17.1	20.2
One woman, one man	73.4	61.3
Other	1.3	1.3
All mortgages (000s)	6846	10,410

Source: CSO (1995) Social Focus on Women, Table 3.8, p.38.

owners. Women will have less income available for buying a house, and are at greater risk of being unable to sustain a mortgage. Single never-married women are less likely than single never-married men to be buying their own homes: 37 per cent of single men are buying their own homes with a mortgage, compared with 27 per cent of single women who are doing so (Table 7.1). Nevertheless, an increasing proportion of mortages are held by women only; in 1994 over 17 per cent of mortgages were held by women only, more than double the proportion in 1983 (Table 7.3), showing that women's independent access to home ownership is increasing as a proportion of all households.

Women and the private rented sector

The private rented sector presents special problems for women: high cost, low quality of housing, insecurity of tenure, risk of harassment by landlords and by other tenants, and lack of support. Market mechanisms also govern access to private rented housing, though different mechanisms are at work than for home ownership. Renting private housing depends on its availability, quality and cost. Despite efforts by recent government housing policies to halt the decline of the private rented sector, it has continued its long term decline. In 1971, 20 per cent of households were renting privately, but by 1995 the size of this sector had halved; only 10 per cent of households lived in private rented accommodation (Office for

National Statistics 1997, p.29). Thus opportunities to secure private rented housing have declined generally. However, government housing policies that deregulated rents and security of tenure (Housing Act 1988 and Housing (Scotland) Act 1988) have also had an effect on the cost and supply of private rented housing. This remains an important housing market, though, particularly for single person households (see Table 7.1), housing 23 per cent of single men and 21 per cent of single women. The condition of housing in the private rented sector is the worst in the UK. A review of the condition of UK housing (Leather and Morrison 1997) found that one in five homes in the private rented sector was unfit. It also found that it was people on low incomes who lived in poor housing, especially those over 75 and young people at the beginning of their housing careers. Although younger men are more likely than younger women to live in poor housing, the position reverses with age. Over the age of 30, households headed by women are more likely to live in substandard housing (14% of those aged 40-59) (Leather and Morrison 1997).

Once private rented housing is achieved, women may have difficulty sustaining access to this form of housing, due to harassment by landlords (Watson with Austerberry 1986), insecurity of tenure and problems of the affordability of market rents. Woods reports that women in private rented housing suffer higher rates of harassment and poor living conditions than men and that a 1983/84 study (1996, p.74) found that 12 per cent of women living on their own in private rented housing in London were victims of sexual harassment.

Women-headed households

Single women

Young single women experience greater barriers than young single men in securing access to home ownership and to social renting. Their relatively poorer earning power will reduce their borrowing capacity and their ability to cross the entry price threshold for home owership. Woods, supported by statistics collected by the Department of the Environment in 1993, argues that single female households are less likely to buy into owner occupation than single men: 43 per cent of single men are buying on a mortgage, compared with 22 per cent of single women (Woods 1996, p.69), although as Table 7.3 shows, the gap between the proportion of single men and single women obtaining mortgages may be narrowing. While the rate of access to home ownership for women may be improving, paying for home ownership can mean considerable financial hardship. Women's lower earnings mean that women spend a higher proportion of their income than men on housing. Woods (1996, p.71) argues, drawing on the analysis by Muir and Ross (1993) of women's average wages and the lowest decile of London house prices, that only 15 per cent of women in London could afford to buy a house even at the lowest end of the housing market.

All single people experience barriers in securing access to social rented housing since allocation policies tend to give priority to households with children or with a 'vulnerable' adult.

Some young women who are discharged from care will need some form of supported accommodation in order to help them to make the transition to independence and to sustain a tenancy.

Particular housing difficulties may arise for older single women carers after the caring relationship ends, perhaps on the death of a parent. If they had been living with a dependent parent in social rented housing in which the tenancy was in the parent's name, unless they can succeed to the tenancy to their parent's house, they may face the prospect of homelessness immediately after the loss of a parent.

Lone parents

There has been a great deal of debate about lone parenthood generally and, in particular, the extent to which single women become mothers in order to secure a council house. While there is no evidence to support the view that single women become pregnant in order to secure a council house, it is very clear that lone parents, and lone mothers in particular, are highly reliant on social rented housing. This is due to both push and pull factors: partly because of the substantial difficulties lone parents face in securing owner occupied housing and partly due to allocation policies in the social rented housing sectors which allocate housing according to need rather than the ability to pay. Lone parents (and lone mothers especially) are less than half as likely to be owner occupiers (35%) than other families with dependent children (77%) (Office of Population Census and Surveys 1997, p.25) and more than three times as likely to be renting housing from a local authority or housing association (54%) compared with 17 per cent of other families with dependent children who live in social rented housing. Single, never married mothers, are especially reliant on social rented housing, as Table 7.4 shows, since more than two-thirds live in social rented housing. It is also worth highlighting the high proportion of concealed households for this group, an example of hidden homelessness which would not be evident in local authority homelessness statistics.

Lone parents also experience high levels of housing insecurity. There is a disproportionately high number of lone parents amongst younger households in the social rented sector who have been found to move house most often.

While allocation of council housing is made by reference to housing need, women's access in this sector can depend on their status as mothers, and whether their children live with them. Lone mothers in particular are at risk of falling into the housing benefit trap, in which each pound earned from employment results in an almost equivalent reduction in housing benefit, so that there is for many lone parents a trade-off between maintaining access to housing and taking on paid employment and reducing dependency on means-tested benefits.

Table 7.4: Lone parents and their housing tenure

England	Percentage of households			
	LA or HA tenant	owner occupied	concealed families	private tenants
never married	68	6	16	10
formerly married	48	40	3	9
lone fathers	26	50	11	12

Source: Green, Hazel and Jacqui Hansboro (1995), p.98

Older women

Many older women are widows living in their former matrimonial homes, and own their homes outright (having paid off the mortgage). While it might appear superficially that they are well housed, this is not the case for many older widows. Since their incomes can be very low, there may be insufficient resources to heat their homes adequately, so that 'adequate' housing may be unsustainable because of fuel poverty. They may also experience difficulties in maintaining their properties to a satisfactory standard; elderly owner occupiers' houses have some of the worst problems of disrepair.

Demographic change, and in particular, the growth in the numbers of women over 75 has incresed the need for supported accommodation, without the supply of such housing keeping pace. Owner occupied sheltered housing has the same problems of access for those disadvantaged in the labour market. Older women who may need sheltered housing may not be able to afford it.

Lesbians

Lesbians are invisible in housing policy and practice. Because there is at the heart of housing policy an assumption that a 'family' consists of a heterosexual couple with any of their children, it may be difficult for lesbian couples to have their housing need acknowledged since there is scant recognition that lesbian couples may wish to gain access to housing as a single household unit. Since lesbian couples are unlikely to receive priority under social rented housing allocation rules, they are more likely to find housing in the private rented sector or as owner occupiers. In private rented housing, they risk harassment by landlords and other tenants. Further difficulties can arise when relationships break down (Smailes 1994).

Housing and relationship breakdown

The risk of losing access to home ownership when marriages or relationships break down can be high for both men and women. Compared with a rate of 79 per cent for married couples, the rate of home ownership for divorced and separated people with a mortgage falls to 37 per cent for men and 38 per cent for women who are divorced or separated (Table 7.1). If women remain in owner occupation after divorce, they often face financial difficulty in continuing to pay a mortgage (Symon 1990; McCarthy and Simpson 1991; Bull 1993). Access to home ownership will decrease and the cost of owner occupied housing after relationship breakdown will increase for some women as a result of the Child Support Act 1991, since the Act reduces the financial incentives for former partners to give over all or part of their share in the equity of the former matrimonial home (Wasoff and Morris 1996).

Moving to cheaper owner occupied accommodation can also be difficult. Indirect discrimination by financial institutions (usually through earnings assessments and requirements for unbroken, secure, full-time work patterns) in granting a mortgage to separated and divorced women reduces opportunities to move house within the owner occupied sector following relationship breakdown. Thus the policies of social landlords are crucial for the housing security of women and children following relationship breakdown.

Table 7.5: Women's housing tenure after divorce

Tenure of women's (aged 20 to 59) accommodation one year after divorce by tenure of the former matrimonial home, 1991–1993		
Great Britain	**Tenure of former matrimonial home**	
	Percentage	
tenure one year after divorce	owner occupied	rented
owner occupied, owned outright	10	1
owner occupied with mortgage	57	6
rented from local authority, new town or housing association	11	67
other rented	5	11
not a householder	18	16

Source: CSO (1995) Social Focus on Women, Table 1.8, p.12

Table 7.5 gives some indication of the housing transitions triggered by divorce and relationship breakdown, although these data will underestimate the extent of housing mobility for women on divorce, since there will also be substantial housing change *within* each housing tenure. Only 67 per cent of divorced women who were living in owner occupied housing whilst married were still living in this housing tenure one year after divorce. One-third moved into rented housing or were no longer independent householders.

Women, housing and domestic violence

Where a relationship breakdown is associated with domestic violence social services may be involved to protect the interests of women and/or their children. Women may wish either to remain in their homes and to exclude their violent partner, or, if this is not possible, safe or desirable, to move to another home. Thus, sustaining access to housing where there has been domestic violence may entail excluding a violent partner or moving to alternative accommodation. Failure in either of these can lead to homelessness (Morley 1993). Relationship breakdown, whether violent or non-violent, accounted for one-third of all homeless households accepted by Scottish local authorities (see Table 7.6).

Legal remedies to oust a violent spouse were introduced by legislation such as the Matrimonial Homes (Family Protection) (Scotland) Act 1981 and the Domestic Violence (Matrimonial Proceedings) Act 1976. In principle, these should have

Table 7.6: Why do people become homeless?

Reason	England 1991 (%)	Scotland 1994/5 (%)
Parents/relatives/friends cannot accommodate	42	35
Relationship breakdown (violent and non-violent)	16	33
Mortgage arrears/ reposesssion	11	3
Rent arrears/eviction/loss of service tenancy	2	3
Other	29	26

Note: these figures are for households accepted as homeless or potentially homeless.
Source: DoE Homeless Statistics 1992, Scottish Office Housing Statistical Bulletin, May

helped women experiencing domestic violence to sustain occupation of the matrimonial home by excluding their violent spouse. However, in practice, these remedies are often ineffective in their enforcement and little used by most women who need them, thereby reducing women's housing security in response to violence in the home.

Finding alternative accommodation presents barriers encountered by all women on relationship breakdown, although there is the safety net of homelessness provision. Under current legislative provisions, women experiencing violence or the risk of violence from someone in their household are classified as homeless. If they have children or are pregnant, they are also deemed to be in priority need. This places a duty on the local authority to whom they apply to ensure that accommodation is made available to them. However, the safety net of homelessness legislation is a weak one; women may face long periods in substandard temporary accommodation and there is no obligation on local authorities to ensure that the standard of accommodation that is made available will be satisfactory.

Women and homelessness

Homelessness can be seen as the most extreme form of failure to secure access to housing. Homelessness has grown steadily since the primary statutes, the Housing (Homeless Persons) Act 1977, and subsequent legislation were introduced. The National Audit Office found that from 1979 to 1989, the number of households accepted as homeless doubled to 126,000. Now it is even more. Over a quarter of a million people–over 140,000 households–are now officially recognised as homeless in England in 1991/92, and local authorities have accepted they must provide them with permanent accommodation. The same trend is found in Scotland, as Table 7.7 shows, where the rate of homelessness has more than doubled since 1984.

One measure of women's difficulties in getting access to housing can be found in the homelessness statistics, which show that women-headed households predominate amongst homeless households (Morley and Pascall 1996). Lone parents are at particular risk of homelessness, accounting for 43 per cent of those accepted as homeless in 1994 (Pascall 1997, p.147). Moreover, these statistics underestimate the scale of homelessness for women, since they will not reflect the true extent of hidden homelessness or homelessness amongst single women.

Table 7.7: Homeless households in Scotland: 1984/85 and 1994/95

Local authority assessment	1984/85	%	1994/95	%
Total applicants	20,478		41,500	
Priority homeless	10,708	52	17,400	42
Non-priority homeless	2672	13	14,100	34
Not homeless	1866	9	5300	13
Not stated/lost contact	7098	26	10,000	11

Source: Scottish Office Statistical Bulletin (Housing Series), (May 1996) Table 1, p.5.

Homelessness has been the route to obtaining local authority housing for many women, rather than being allocated a house after being on the waiting list, which shows the growth in acute housing need. Women-headed households are not only disproportionately represented amongst homeless households, they are more likely to cite relationship breakdown and violence as the immediate reasons for their homelessness (Table 7.6). Thus problems in gender relationships cause housing hardship for women.

Conclusion

This chapter has offered an overview of a variety of issues in housing policy and provision which will affect many women users of social services. It has considered the ways in which women's disadvantage in the labour market and position in the family result in housing disadvantage and difficulties in obtaining and sustaining access to housing. Each of the main housing tenures have their own characteristic means of getting access to housing, and therefore their own problems for women. While social rented housing has issues of access to good quality housing for women, it nevertheless provides a safety net for the wider housing system. Women-headed households exemplify the difficulties all women face in securing independent access to housing. Policies which erode the provision and quality of social rented housing reduce all women's housing opportunities, housing security and social rights of citizenship.

References

Bull, J. (1993) *Housing Consequences of Relationship Breakdown.* Department of the Environment, London: HMSO.

Central Statistical Office (CSO) (1995) *Social Focus on Women.* Central Statistical Office, London: HMSO.

Leather, P. and Morrison (1997) *The State of UK Housing: A Factfile on Dwelling Conditions.* Bristol: The Policy Press.

McCarthy, P. and Simpson, B. (1991) *Issues in Post-Divorce Housing.* Aldershot: Avebury.

Morley, R. and Pascall, G. (1996) 'Women and homelessness: proposals from the Department of the Environment – II domestic violence.' *Journal of Social Welfare and Family Law 18,* 3, 327–340.

Morris, J. and Winn, M. (1990) *Housing and Social Inequality.* Harlow: Longman.

Muir, J. and Ross, M. (1993) *Housing the Poorer Sex.* London: London Housing Unit.

Munro, M. and Madigan, R. (1993) 'Privacy in the private sphere.' *Housing Studies 8,* 1, 29–45.

Office for National Statistics (ONS) (1997) *Living in Britain: Results from the 1995 General Household Survey.* London: HMSO.

Office of Population Census and Surveys (OPCS) (1997) *General Household Survey 1995.* Office of Population Census and Surveys, London: HMSO.

Pascall, G. (1997) *Social Policy: A New Feminist Analysis.* London: Routledge.

Sefton, T. (1997) *The Changing Distribution of the Social Wage.* STICERD Occasional Paper 21, London: London School of Economics.

Smailes, J. (1994) 'The struggle has never been simply about bricks and mortar: Lesbians' experience of housing.' In R. Gilroy and R. Woods (eds) *Housing Women.* London: Routledge.

Symon, P. (1990) 'Marital breakdown, gender and home ownership: the owner occupied home in separation and divorce.' In P. Symon (ed) *Housing and Divorce.* Glasgow: Centre for Housing Research.

Wasoff, F. and Morris, S. (1996) 'The Child Support Act: a victory for women?' In J. Millar and H. Jones (eds) *The Politics of the Family.* Aldershot: Avebury.

Watson, S. and Austerberry, H. (1986) *Housing and Homelessness: A Feminist Perspective.* London: Routledge Kegan Paul.

Woods, R. (1994) 'Introduction.' In R. Gilroy and R. Woods (eds) *Housing Women.* London: Routledge.

Woods, R. (1996) 'Women and housing.' In C. Hallett (ed) *Women and Social Policy.* London: Harvester Wheatsheaf.

CHAPTER 8

Race, Culture, Housing and Social Services

Mono Chakrabarti

Persistent discrimination and disadvantage based on the colour of the skin in housing markets has been well documented. Allocation of housing provision for black and minority ethnic populations validated by racial stereotype within the institutional frameworks appears to confirm negative bias in publicly rented and owner-occupied tenures (Dalton 1991; Sanne and Skellington 1989). In this chapter we will locate the reasons for these states of affairs which severely affect a significant number of black British people. There will also be discussion of how information about accessing housing provision is managed by providers, and the experience of minority ethnic people in relation to public sector service provision like housing and social work. The impact of legislation, in particular the Race Relations Act 1976, on the distribution of public sector housing will be further examined.

In order to understand racial discrimination in the context of housing and social work one needs to take on board the historical significance of the migration processes of black and minority ethnic people. For many hundreds of years Britain systematically extended her colonial and imperial power to cover all corners of the globe. By the end of the last century, Britain ruled an Empire that included over one-fifth of the world's population. Many British subjects were not white and were forced to produce wealth for the benefit of the 'motherland'.

This process of wealth accumulation, which resulted in the economic and social exploitation of the Indian sub-continent, Africa and other parts of the Empire, helped to make the Industrial Revolution possible in Britain. This complete economic and human subjugation was justified by defining black people as inferior semi-humans. Out of this social mindset institutions have evolved which have had the effect of transmitting attitudes and beliefs of racial superiority and practices of racial oppression from one generation to another (Chakrabarti 1991).

As far as Britain was concerned however, until the Second World War the manifestations of racial discrimination–due to lack of proximity–were largely contained outside the British Isles, and its true internal reality only became clear during the post-war period. The entrenched racial inequalities in housing and other public sectors were sown through politicians' dogged insistence that racism was alien to the British character and by an ill founded but politically convenient assumption that early patterns of segregation and the housing problems embedded in them, could best be solved by immigration controls. However, recently released Cabinet papers tell a different tale. The government of the immediate post-war period did everything it could to recruit immigrant workers from anywhere but the 'New Commonwealth'. It preferred displaced European workers from Germany, Austria and East European refugees and anyone else who the Royal Commission on Population (1949) could be sure 'were of good human stock and not prevented by their religion or race from intermarrying with the host population and becoming merged with it'.

The government wanted workers who would not compound the 'threat' of ghettos becoming established in port areas and who would be more 'fitted' than 'colonial peoples' to the kinds of jobs available. In the end the demands of the economy won the day and people from colonies and ex-colonies were invited in as cheap labour with a promise of a better life.

It can be seen from this that racism and the disadvantage which follows from it is not just a belief system or set of attitudes. It is an ideology that is reinforced by those who hold economic and social power and it affects housing, social work, education, media, and the family, as well as individuals (Sivannandan 1982). Thus it could be argued that racism is not the outcome of racial prejudice, but rather that prejudice is shaped and articulated by racism.

Housing, race and the law

Before moving on to look at the housing profile, and knowledge and use of housing services from a minority ethnic perspective, it is important to consider the implications of legislation for housing and social services provision.

In view of the lack of up-to-date information on service provision in local authority departments, the Commission for Racial Equality (CRE) decided in 1989 to conduct a detailed survey to identify progress made on the development and implementation of equal opportunity policies in the provision and delivery of services.

The survey identified that nearly two-thirds of the 116 departments in England, Scotland and Wales do not have written equal opportunity policies to cover the delivery and provision of services to black and minority ethnic communities. This was a matter for great concern, as most of the departments covered in this survey were in locations with a substantial minority ethnic population. Those departments which had equal opportunity policies in employment were more likely to have considered equal opportunity measures in the provision of services. A key issue raised by the survey was the need for a formal written policy, rather than simply a general intention to treat all service users fairly. It was argued that it was not good enough simply to have good intentions; what was needed was a specific written policy, the implementation of which could be systematically monitored and regularly revised.

In these circumstances, a great deal of work is required if local authority departments and housing associations are to fulfil their obligations under the race relations legislation and provide services free from racial discrimination. Equally important in a multi-racial society is that authorities carry a responsibility to provide services that are appropriate to identified needs.

The Act of 1976 contains many provisions that are directly relevant to housing and social services managers in formulating their strategic thinking and planning in the delivery of service provision. The most important section of the Act in respect of service provision is Section 20. This makes it unlawful for anyone concerned with the provision of goods, facilities or services to the public (or a section of the public) to discriminate on racial grounds by refusing or deliberately omitting to provide them, or as regards their quality or the manner in which or the terms on which they are provided. This discrimination may be direct, for example, less favourable treatment, or indirect, that is applying a requirement or condition which has a disproportionately adverse effect on a particular racial group, and which cannot be justified.

Section 71 of the Act places a duty on every local authority to make appropriate arrangements with a view to ensuring that its various functions are carried out with due regard to the need to eliminate unlawful racial discrimination and to promote equality of opportunity and good relations between persons of different racial groups.

Sections 37 and 38 of the Race Relations Act promote positive measures for the encouragement of employees who are members of a particular racial group to take up training or employment, where that racial group is under-represented. However, discrimination at the point of selection is not permissible under these sections of the Act. Similarly, Section 5 (2) (d) of the Act allows the appointment of a member of a particular racial group where the holder of the job concerned provides persons of that racial group with personal services promoting their welfare, and those services can most effectively be provided by a person of that racial group.

The Code of Practice in Rented Housing (CRE 1991) provides guidance as to the manner in which the Act should be applied in relation to housing provision. The Code does not carry the authority of courts and tribunals, but does have a bearing in that guidance provided in the Code is admissible in evidence in any proceedings under the Race Relations Act and 'if any provision appears to be relevant to a question arising in the proceedings, it must be taken into account in determining that question' (CRE 1991, p.1).

The effectiveness of the Act and its enforcement agency, the Commission for Racial Equality, could be said to be problematic (Forbes 1988). One of the major shortcomings of the Act is its failure to impose strong enough pressure on employers and service providers to monitor their practices in order to obtain compliance in the short term (MacEwan 1995). But although the Act may not be perfect, it does carry substantial weight and provides a comprehensive coverage incorporating both public and private sectors.

Specific legislation regarding race and social work provision can be illustrated through the Children (Scotland) Act 1995 which came into force in April 1997, and which places a duty on local authorities to prepare, to publish and to review constantly plans for the comprehensive provision of services to children in their area. This shall be carried out by co-ordinating various service departments including housing within local authorities. They must do this in consultation with children and parents who use the services, other agencies involved with children and voluntary agencies and organisations.

In Part II of the Act specific recognition was given for the first time to the significance of the racial, religious, cultural and linguistic needs of Scotland's children. Sections 17, 22 and 95 impose a duty on local authorities to have regard to a child's religious persuasion, racial origin, cultural and linguistic background; when a child has been 'looked after', in 'need' of welfare provision and issues related to 'adoption' of a child.

This duty is set within the context of a number of principles underpinning the Act. These include support for families, shared responsibilities with parents, corporate responsibilities within local authorities, collaboration between agencies and most importantly the paramouncy principle. This states that the welfare of the child is the paramount consideration when significant decisions are being made. With respect to this, issues of religion, racial origin, and cultural and linguistic background are crucial. They are central to a child's life experience, heritage and identity. They are also integral to understanding and establishing children's needs. Practitioners and policy makers need to give thoughtful consideration to these factors whenever they are carrying out their duties to safeguard and promote the overall welfare of children from a minority ethnic background.

Under all the above legislative framework, it is possible for housing and social services management to take a strategic position in developing appropriate services and structures for minority ethnic communities.

Tenure patterns and the use of housing services

In 1983 the Policy Studies Institute carried out a detailed survey of the position of black people including their housing needs in Britain (Brown 1984). The study found that minority ethnic and black people tend to live in older buildings. White households have, on average, twice the amount of space per person available to Asian households and over one and a half times that available to people from Afro-Caribbean background. Twelve per cent of Asian households were overcrowded. A large number of people from minority ethnic background were forced into buying substandard houses. Unfortunately, the situation has not changed or improved very much since that large scale study by the Policy Studies Institute. In a recent study (Madood 1997) involving 8063 individual interviews covering all parts of the UK, the researcher found that the incidence and prevalence of racial disadvantage have not shifted to any significant extent.

Evidence suggests that there is a very low take up of public sector housing including special needs provision by minority ethnic people (Ahmed and Atkin 1996; Brailey 1991). Community based housing associations have also failed to live up to their declared policy of equal access to their housing stock from minority ethnic communities. Barriers created to access to housing provision both in terms of application processing and allocation systems operated by housing associations tend to indicate that so far they have hurled more obstacles into the stream (Brown 1996). A number of reasons could be identified for such a pattern:

1. lack of appropriate information about the available services

2. inappropriateness of existing provision, for example, size of accommodation and location of it

3. vulnerability of minority ethnic residents to the risk of being racially abused

4. lack of ethnic monitoring by service providers with the consequent scope for discrimination

5. relative absence of black and ethnic minority employees in the agencies of service providers.

A large scale study carried out in the Central belt of Scotland has once again confirmed that in spite of significant legislative changes (for example, Race Relations Act 1976; Children Act 1989, and NHS and Community Care Act 1989, and publicly proclaimed better understanding of the nature of multi-racial society), the experience of minority ethnic people in housing and social services still remains significantly problematic (Campbell 1996).

The research team carried out extensive interviews with 204 ethnic minority home owners and 106 white home owners. Consistent with national trends, they found that minority ethnic households were more likely to live in extended family groups, with an average household size of 4.5 compared to a household size of 2.7 in the comparison group.

Members of such households were also more likely to be self-employed, or not working because they were unemployed, sick, disabled or looking after the family; they were less likely to be in full or part-time paid employment. The study further identified that minority ethnic householders often felt forced into owner occupation because of a perceived lack of suitable alternatives. They also faced a more limited choice of houses to buy and lived in poorer, crowded conditions and homes needing major repairs. Minority ethnic owners found the experience more difficult than white owners, from arranging a mortgage to finding a suitable house within the preferred location and price range.

This study along with other similar research (Askham, Henshaw and Tarpey 1995) has identified that minority ethnic groups face more limited housing opportunities, and poorer housing conditions than the general population. Many turn to owner occupation because they have been unable to satisfy their housing needs in other tenures. While owner occupation tends to be an aspirational move for many minority ethnic people it may not be their tenure of choice, and may not provide the desired solution to their perceived housing needs.

The authors conclude that housing providers in formulating policy options should consider a number of key issues in a strategic manner, such as:

1. improving access to alternative housing options for minority ethnic groups, especially within public sector housing.

2. provision of appropriate advice acknowledging the value of informal networks amongst minority ethnic communities about the range of housing options, and assistance in accessing them.

3. provision of targeted advice and information to minority ethnic groups on improvement and repair grants and take up of other benefits.

4. in the medium to longer term, care must be taken to incorporate the housing needs of minority ethnic groups into the strategic and physical planning process through sustained consultation with minority ethnic community groups.

Racial abuse and harassment

A study in 1990 involving 400 individuals from black and minority ethnic communities found that 88.1 per cent of minority ethnic people asked experienced racial abuse. Fifty per cent stated that they were abused daily and 52.4 per cent of the sample had experienced some form of racially motivated physical attack (Bowes *et al.* 1990).

Minority ethnic people who have reported incidents of racial harassment to the police, housing and social services departments in the hope that these authorities would be sympathetic are too often met with complacency or disbelief by the authorities. Given these attitudes of institutional racism few people now consider it worth while to file official complaints. Consequently, the official recording of racially motivated incidents maintained by the police and housing departments misrepresents the prevalence of racism.

Another study (Dalton 1990) revealed that most minority ethnic people were unaware of their entitlement to various housing benefits and were apprehensive about the service they would receive as applicants for public sector housing. Key problems identified were:

1. lack of information in languages other than English

2. an allocations policy which enforced dispersal of minority ethnic families to the peripheral schemes

3. covertly racist tenants associations

4. staff who seemed impatient and unsympathetic, particularly when confronted with allegations of racially motivated abuse by other tenants.

Both the studies concluded that the housing authorities failed in their obligation to provide a non-discriminatory service.

It is not surprising then that very often minority ethnic communities feel that public agencies are incapable of dealing with complaints of racial harassment contrary to their publicly proclaimed position regarding equal opportunities policy. As it is normally the victims of racial harassment who are moved, the fact that it takes such a long time to get a housing transfer compounds the whole negative experience. While the process of housing transfer is long, the endurance of racial harassment for many minority ethnic individuals is even longer. Therefore, the adoption of equal opportunities policies alone may have no beneficial impact on the delivery of services to minority communities and moreover, the commitment and interest of professionals in the absence of effective policy and managerial support makes very limited impact.

Social services and ethnicity

The cumulative picture which emerged in Britain by the middle of the 1990s was one which suggested that many of the sources of discrimination for black and minority ethnic service users were broadly similar in pattern, both in impeding access to existing services and in hindering the development of services adapted to the needs of minority groups. By and large a whole range of legislation gives local authorities and public agencies the primary role in challenging existing patterns of discriminatory service provision. This presupposes a collaborative approach involving social services, housing, education, leisure and recreation and other services working together in order to formulate appropriate policy options reflecting the multi-racial and multi-cultural nature of British society. With local government under continuous attack from central government for lack of direction, it is more important than ever to know what we are defending. Without such a critical awareness, vulnerability to backlash will inevitably be increased. In that context the joint planning and service delivery provisions under a number of statutes like National Health Service and Community Care Act 1990 and the English and the Scottish Children Acts of 1989 and 1995 provide an opportunity to address the issues of discrimination and disadvantage based on skin colour. The legal requirement to prepare and publish regular plans following full consultation with interested members of the public and service users does provide a real scope for social services and housing to look at issues of discrimination and deficiencies in service provision more systematically and in a co-ordinated manner (Macey 1995).

In this section an attempt will be made to identify concern that, not withstanding those legislative requirements, a large and increasing range of black and minority ethnic people's needs are not being met or else are being met inappropriately by social services in general. As has already been said with regard to institutionalised attitudes and beliefs, racism poses a considerable challenge in Britain today, and in particular to social work in a multi-racial community, surpassing unemployment and poverty in importance among the minority ethnic population, because it is the cause of these further social ills. The problems reviewed in this section are directly relevant to the adequacy of how social workers address the housing and shelter needs of black and Asian service users.

Social work is thus faced with a dilemma. On the one hand, the profession and its organisation are part and parcel of the process of institutionalised racism, with which black people are at odds. Yet, on the other hand, the profession is fundamentally concerned to support minority groups in their struggle to survive in this discriminatory society, and to ensure as far as possible that society does provide for groups' welfare in the context of current legislative requirements. This dilemma was succinctly expressed in a slightly different context by Younghusband (1970), who argued that, of all the professions, social workers are particularly closely engaged with individuals and societal problems and are involved with the practical realisation of 'the great democratic ideal of liberty, equality and justice in all its complexities' (p.17).

Social work is practised and taught in different settings in formal and informal organisations, both large and small, and with diverse organisational goals, but the effect of racial disadvantage remains equally damaging as far as minority ethnic groups are concerned irrespective of the setting.

It has been argued by a number of writers that social services organisations and social work teaching departments have been slow to consider the need to change their practice in a multi-racial society (Aluffi-Pentioni and Lorenz 1996; Fernando 1995). There are two main reasons for this lack of appropriate response. The first is that traditional social work approaches may not be relevant for people of non-western origin with different traditions of value and concepts of welfare. In the European context special emphasis is given to a service user's individuality and to his or her own right to self-determination. In accord with this basic tenet of social work theory, the social worker uses intervention methods to perform a facilitating role, enabling the individual to reach his or her own decision about how a problem can be best resolved and to act accordingly.

A second reason why social work had failed to adapt to multi racial communities is that on the whole, insufficient effort has been made to identify unexpressed or poorly articulated need (Patel 1990). Moreover, as Dalrymple and Burke (1995) have suggested, there is a contradiction in social work practice in the sense that in the cases of Asian and Afro-Caribbean clients, the view is often taken that problems emanate from features within minority ethnic people's social and cultural background. By adopting this perspective social workers see the problem as being beyond their influence or control and, in consequence, regard it as not requiring their intervention.

Establishing precisely which problems fall within the realms of social work creates difficulties, not only among social workers themselves, but also between social work and other welfare agencies. More recently, however, concern about differences of perceptions has focused not so much on inter-agency relations, but on the relationship between social workers themselves and their minority ethnic clients. The possible perception by clients of social workers as agents of social control, may lead to difficulties, especially if the social workers are seen as purveyors of a dominant British culture and tradition. This difficulty has led some writers to suggest that social work with minority groups should focus on the relativity of value systems and the extent to which these are culturally and religiously determined (Dean and Khan 1997). It raises an interesting question as to whose value system should prevail, that of social workers or that of clients.

Social work with minority ethnic people also operates through two channels which influence client–worker relationships. Dominelli (1989) identifies these as *exclusion* and *inclusion* channels. The exclusion mode operates through a mechanism of limiting access to service provisions from minority groups. For instance, it is now well documented that minority ethnic clients do not get their fair share of home helps, meals-on-wheels or places in residential or sheltered accommodation (e.g. Chakrabarti and Cadman 1997).

The inclusion channel, or over-representation of black and minority clients in child care or mental health services, reinforces the preconceived view that minority groups are 'troublesome'. By taking a colour blind approach social workers may deny clients' special experience of themselves. The traditional view that everybody should be treated in the same way inevitably leads to inequality and injustice specifically in relation to service outcome.

Another factor that the providers of social work services very seldom take into account is the demography of the black and minority population in the country. As with all other public service provision, a lack of understanding of the nature and composition of minority ethnic groups will inevitably lead to wrong or inappropriate policy formulation, which in turn will produce more dissatisfaction and injustice. For example, in the UK nearly 45 per cent of minority people are under 15 years old, compared to around 25 per cent of the population as a whole. At the other end of age structure, only 11 per cent are over retirement age–the overall national figure being around 19 per cent (Social Trends 1996). However, this particular situation will significantly change in the early part of the 21st century, and it appears that very few public institutions are anywhere near taking this demographic factor into serious consideration in the context of relevant policy formulation. For example, will social work and housing departments be able to develop appropriate support systems for the increasing number of service seekers from minority ethnic communities?

In the past, social services either adopted the 'colour blind' approach by maintaining that they treat all people equally or argued that they were fulfilling their obligations, for example, by appointing a few black social workers or white workers who had developed specialist interest in dealing with minority issues. Research on community care and housing has also often betrayed a similar 'colour blind' approach. A useful overview of 21 research projects carried out between 1991 and 1996 (Watson 1997) included only one study (Radia 1996) that specifically addressed issues of housing and community care for an ethnic minority group.

Pressure from the minority ethnic communities has caused some agencies to understand the inadequacy of their approaches and to begin looking systematically at 'race' issues in social work. Pressure has also been growing for agencies to do more to ensure that minority ethnic people make full use of all their services, for example, by translating information leaflets, providing interpreters and publicising service provision through community based minority organisations. Scandinavian countries, in particular Sweden, guarantee all legal residents the right to learn their own language, culture and heritage. It has been recognised that a varied culture and heritage can only enhance and enrich Swedish society and a pluralistic perspective is the only path to take to make a society civilised.

Social work education and training and black and minority ethnic people

The 'race' dimension in social work education is fragmentary and incomplete, often inconsequential, and varies from region to region. A probable consequence of this can be seen in the results of analysis carried out in Scotland, which has indicated that by and large social workers are not confident and are ill-equipped to work with and provide support for people from minority communities (Cadman and Chakrabarti 1992). This is in spite of all the regulatory expectations of the Central Council for Education and Training in Social Work, the statutory body which carries the validating responsibility of all social work courses in the United Kingdom.

Examining how social work courses prepare students to develop an anti-racist perspective, Naik (1990) identified three broad approaches. The first approach Naik called a 'technical' perspective. It emphasises equality of opportunity for all students and is concerned with the achievement of black and minority ethnic students. Curriculum change is seen as improving basic skills but within a compensatory approach.

Second, there is the 'moral' approach to curriculum building in social work. This model aims to reduce prejudice and discrimination and to replace it with a positive approach. The emphasis here is on materials and the use of literature to initiate student discussion and to sensitise them to the 'race' dimension in its ideological context.

The last approach is what he calls the 'socio–political' perspective, which is by no means universal in usage in social work courses. It implies a shift in value consensus in society to the belief that a plural society of relatively separate but equal groups will emerge. Those committed to the idea do wish to permeate the whole curriculum with a multi-racial and multi-cultural emphasis and may offer their students skills with which to assist their clients. Those who support this approach give precedence to the identity, needs and aspirations of the minority ethnic groups.

It has been argued by many community based ethnic minority organisations that there is a need to re-affirm the prominence of minority ethnic people's needs throughout social work training, recognising that their disproportionately limited demand for services is in itself a significant indicator of racially prejudiced practice. There is also a need to ensure that a black anti-racist perspective is maintained throughout teaching in predominantly or exclusively white educational centres. In many cases, such institutions may need to take more active steps to recruit black and minority ethnic teachers and students. Additional and intensive training to overcome the deficient practice base of many teachers in this area will be crucial.

It will significantly improve their teaching perspective if contributions are sought from ethnic minority organisations representing black and minority groups. But if this approach is to be effective it will require an understanding of how these organisations operate and the development of a sustained partnership on an equal basis without the potential for exploitation.

The methods for developing and demonstrating through practice what anti-racist and ethnically sensitive practice means in the context of predominantly white agencies require examination. At the level of demonstrating an effective awareness of anti-racist issues, social work practice placement offers opportunities for analysing how agency policy, procedures and practice traditions impact on minority groups and individuals. However, the opportunity to demonstrate ethnically sensitive practice is effectively curtailed unless work with black and minority ethnic people can be undertaken at some stage in social workers' training.

Conclusion

Only comparatively recently have social welfare institutions and policy makers begun to realise how much of a myth their image of service provision devoid of racially moderated practices is. At the level of experience of racism, black and minority ethnic people's positions are no less horrifying than those reported elsewhere in Europe. At the level of institutional racism, the policies, procedure and practices of public services, whether the housing, social work services or police, are not significantly different as experienced by black and minority ethnic people.

Disadvantage based on colour of skin and ethnicity is manifested in many guises in social work and housing, as the review of some of the current literature has illustrated. A future direction in housing and social work policies and service provisions should incorporate a multi-racial vision and an approach based on inclusion and empowerment of all the communities which reflect diversity in societal composition. The attempt by social work and housing to enhance accessibility to service provision from minority communities should take into account the importance and relevance of consultation because only through listening can 'race' equality be incorporated into service planning.

Work with and appropriate support for minority communities provide a major challenge to housing and social service providers to break out of the *laissez-faire* indifference that exists, to accept our multi-racial society, and to build foundations for its subsequent improvement. Social services can and should be organised in ways which facilitate protection from inequality and maximise developmental potential, but only if they are seen as part of an overall development programme involving both housing and social work optimising welfare for the vulnerable section of the population and not as a short route to ad hoc attempts at amelioration. After all, there is a difference between knowing toothache as a patient and as a dentist.

References

Ahmad, W. and Atkin, K. (1996) *Race and Community Care*. Buckingham: Open University Press.

Aluffi-Pentioni, A. and Lorenz, W. (ed) (1996) *Anti-Racist Work with Young People*. Dorset: Russell House Publishing.

Askham, J., Henshaw, L., and Tarpey, M. (1995) *Social and Health Authority Services for Elderly People from Black and Minority Ethnic Communities*. London: HMSO.

Brailey, M. (1991) 'Ethnic minorities and special needs housing provision.' In A. Bowes and D. Sim (eds) *Demands and Constraints*. Edinburgh: Scottish Council of Voluntary Organisations.

Bowes, A., McLuskey, J. and Sim, D. (1990) *Ethnic Minority Housing Problems*. Glasgow: Glasgow City Council.

Brown, C. (1984) *Black and White Britain*. London: Heinemann.

Brown, V. (1996) 'Racial harassment: action on abuse.' *Housing 32*, 2, 30–33.

Cadman, M. and Chakrabarti, M. (1992) 'Social work in a multi-racial society.' In D. Devine (ed) *One Step Towards Racial Justice*. London: CCETSW.

Campbell, J. (1996) *Constraint and Choice for Minority Ethnic Home Owners in Scotland*. Edinburgh: Heriot-Watt University.

Chakrabarti, M. (1991) *Racial Prejudice*. Buckingham: Open University Press.

Chakrabarti, M. and Cadman, M. (1997) 'Minority ethnic elders in Scotland: facing the challenge.' In D. Sim and A. Bowes (eds) *Ethnic Minorities and Social Welfare Provisions*. Aldershot: Avebury.

Commission for Racial Equality (1991) *Code of Practice in Rented Housing*. London: CRE.

Dalton, M. (1990) *Personal Welfare Services and Ethnic Minorities*. SEMRU.

Dalton, M. (1991) 'Housing association access: achieving racial equality.' In A. Bowes and D. Sim (eds) *Demands and Constraints*. Edinburgh: Scottish Council of Voluntary Organisations.

Dalrymple, J. and Burke, B. (1995) *Anti-Oppressive Practice: Social Care and the Law.* Buckingham: Open University Press.

Dean, H. and Khan, Z. (1997) 'Muslim perspectives on welfare.' *Journal of Social Policy 26,* 2, 193–208.

Dominelli, L. (1989) 'An uncaring profession: an examination of racism in social work.' *New Community 15,* 3, 17–26.

Fernando, S. (1995) *Mental Health in a Multi-ethnic Society.* London: Routledge.

Forbes, D. (1988) *Action on Racial Harassment.* London: Legal Action Group, London Housing Unit.

HMSO (1996) *Social Trends.* London: HMSO.

MacEwan, M. (1995) *Tackling Racism in Europe.* Oxford: Berg Publishers Ltd.

Macey, M. (1995) 'Towards racial justice? A re-evaluation of anti-racism.' *Critical Social Policy 44/45,* 126–146.

Madood, T. (1997) *Ethnic Minorities in Britain.* London: Policy Studies Institute.

Naik, D. (1990) 'An examination of social work education within an anti-racist framework.' Unpublished conference paper.

Patel, N. (1990) *A 'Race' Against Time.* London: Runnymede Trust.

Radia, K. (1996) *Ignored, Silenced, Neglected: Housing and Mental Health Care Needs of Asian People in Four London Boroughs.* York: Joseph Rowntree Foundation.

Royal Commission on Population (1949) *Report of an Inquiry into Family Limitation and its Influence on Human Fertility During the Past Fifty Years.* London: HMSO. Cmd. 7965.

Sanne, P. and Skellington (1989) *Ethnic Minority Housing: Explanations and Policies.* Aldershot: Gower.

Sivannandan, A. (1982) *A Difficult Hunger.* London: Pluto Press.

Younghusband, E. (1970) 'Social work and social values.' *Social Work Today 1,* 6, 5–13.

Watson, L. (1997) *High Hopes: Making Housing and Community Care Work.* York: Joseph Rowntree Foundation.

CHAPTER 9

Discourses and Dilemmas in the Housing and Support Debate

Bridget J. Franklin

The development of community care after the implementation of the National Health Service and Community Care Act of 1990 was initially hampered by the legacy of Griffiths' assertion that the role of housing should be limited to the provision of the 'bricks and mortar' (Griffiths 1988). From the outset this had two effects: it marginalised the involvement of housing organisations in the community care planning process, and it ignored the centrality of appropriate housing in meeting community care objectives. It has taken nearly a decade to mitigate the consequences of those words, and to acknowledge the reality contained in such symbolic and metaphorical rhetoric as housing being the *key* to independent living (DoH 1989) and the *cornerstone* of community care (House of Commons Social Services Committee 1990). This argument having been won, the debate has moved on to an engagement with how housing organisations can be more centrally and effectively involved with planning for community care. This debate has centred on two issues: first, joint planning with the hitherto lead authorities of health and social services (e.g. Allen, Clapham and Franklin 1995; Department of Health 1993; Oldman Chapter 4 in this book; Means and Smith 1994; Spicker 1993) and second, in terms of devising models and strategies to predict the housing need of community care groups at the local level (e.g. Lund and Foord 1997; NFHA 1992; Watson 1996).

There is another area of concern which has arisen within the context of the community care process, but the ramifications of which extend beyond the client group served by the community care process. This relates to the issue of the provision of care and support (see for example Arblaster *et al.* 1996; Clapham and Franklin 1994a and b; Gregory and Brownill 1995; Villeneau 1992). Clearly, the objective of the community care legislation is to enable people to live in the community as opposed to in institutional care settings, and to receive adequate care and support services to enable them to do so. It is for social services departments (or social work departments in Scotland), to identify those who need assistance in the terms of the legislation and, through the community care assessment process, to construct and purchase a package of care which will best meet the needs of the individual concerned. This package of care will then be delivered by one or more of a range of providers, who may be private firms or statutory or voluntary agencies. However, many individuals with care and support needs remain outside the community care system, either because their needs are not complex enough to fall within a cash limited and therefore rationed resource, or who, for one reason or another, do not come into contact with the available services.

Those people who are leaving institutions or hospitals, whether under closure programmes or at the point of discharge after long-term hospitalisation, are those most likely to receive formal packages of care, and are arguably best served by community care. Similarly, those who are in supported accommodation of one type or another are an identified and encapsulated client group whose support needs are likely to be recognised. However, there are many living independently in the community, whose support needs may be no less severe, who tend to be brought to the attention of the relevant authorities only at a time of crisis. Indeed it may be the lack of support which leads them to breaking point. Such people do not include only those in the priority community care groups stipulated in the phraseology of the legislation: *the* elderly, *the* physically disabled, *the* mentally ill and *the* learning disabled. They include also those often subsumed with the former into 'special needs' categories such as ex-offenders, homeless people, women in fear of domestic violence, refugees, young single people, care leavers, lone parents, as well as those described as 'vulnerable', such as people suffering bereavement, those in debt, those who are isolated or afraid, or who simply lack the skills to cope with daily living. All of these people may be struggling to survive unsupported, and yet an awareness of their needs, and the willingness and resources to meet them, might enhance their ability to cope. Very often their housing situation is involved, either because it is some inadequacy in the accommodation which creates a need for support, or because an inability to cope manifests itself in connection with housing, perhaps through nonpayment of rent, neglect of the property, disconnection of utilities, or simply through a request for a transfer to another property. What constitutes support, in these circumstances and others, is an issue which is diffuse and ill-defined, and it is with this issue, and especially with the interface between housing and support, that this chapter is concerned.

Support in the housing context

'Support' is a term used by the caring professions in the context of assisting people in their day-to-day lives when suffering from limitations brought on through ill health, age, disability, life circumstance, personality disorders and so on. Very often it is combined with the term 'care', in the sense that community care is about providing the care and support services that an individual needs to live in the community. As provided in a community care package such care and support can cover a whole spectrum of services from continuous medical and personal care, through to a once-a-week home help. Within the housing literature there is little detailed analysis of the subject of care and support, reflecting the tendency for housing interests to be driven by more pragmatic or policy-led agendas than by theoretical debate. Care and support are therefore issues of concern in relation to their interconnection with the housing situation, rather than as areas to be investigated in terms of their implications for individuals as givers or receivers of care. The literature has been relatively untouched by developments in the feminist critique of social policy where analysis of care has received critical attention (Dalley 1988; Morris 1989; Ungerson 1987).

The words 'care' and 'support' have tended to be used interchangeably in the housing context, although some recent attempts have been made at more precise definitions. Anderson (1994) has attempted to distinguish 'support' from 'care', the latter reflecting the meaning of care as used in the phrase community care, and further divided into medical care (the province of the health service), and social care (the province of the social services). This distinction lies at the heart of one of the failings of community care, in that what should be a 'seamless' service all too often has a ragged gap in the seam between health and social services provision, caused not least by the different responsibilities they are accorded by statute. The notion then of a *continuum* of care, reflecting how an individual might over the course of an episode of disability have a continuum of care needs, is thus lacking. Anderson's conclusion, that support is distinguishable from care, perpetuates the notion of discrete areas to be provided by discrete agencies. In her particular case she is arguing that whilst housing services should not be involved with care, they can, and should, be involved with support. This overlooks the fact that, by her own definition, housing organisations, and especially those providing 'supported' accommodation, often provide social care in addition to support, as will be discussed further below. For the purposes of this chapter, support will be defined as excluding only those elements of care which are transparently medical, such as those involving diagnosis, treatment, prescription of medication, and management of illness or disability (and even these are not always clear cut).

There has been little discussion as to the nature of the functions that should be provided under the aegis of support. Pleace (1995) has suggested that the needs of vulnerable single homeless people can be divided into five categories: housing need, support needs, which include health care and personal support (such as cooking, washing, emotional support and welfare benefits), daily living skills, financial needs and social needs (for relationships and activities). However this categorisation seems somewhat lacking in refinement and its practical application is not made clear.

Watson and Conway (1995) improve on this by examining the support needs which are most likely to be relevant to sustaining independent accommodation, and propose the following list:

- advocacy and advice (to obtain housing and welfare benefits)
- personal assistance (for example with getting up or accompanying to the shops)
- domestic assistance (such as cleaning and meal preparation)
- training in independent living skills (such as budgeting, adequate diet)
- emotional support (which could include counselling)
- support in taking medication
- companionship and social contact
- property management (such as understanding about repairs and adaptations) (Watson and Conway 1995, p.48)

Franklin (forthcoming) addresses the potential support needs of homeless people after they have been given permanent housing, and suggests a categorisation based on the following areas:

- the rehousing process, including the allocation and choosing of property, with the inevitable compromises that have to be made, the equipping of property, the moving in process, and the acceptance of limitations of the property;

- functional skills, including the ability to function effectively in the geographical area, knowing how to use public transport and local facilities, understanding 'the system' in terms of welfare benefits, social services, taxation, the medical system, and the provision of utilities;

- financial skills, including income maximisation, budgeting, comparing prices, dealing with debt; household skills, including cleaning, laundry, shopping, food storage, practical skills such as decorating or changing a plug;

- personal skills, including personal hygiene, taking meals, health care, supervision of medication, appropriate dress and socialising;

- self actualisation, including the development of self-worth and identity, forming relationships, sense of direction, being safe and feeling 'at home'.

The category 'self-actualisation' has been included to reflect the importance users attach to certain ritual or symbolic events which clearly demonstrate the significance of the attainment of self actualisation (Gulstad 1987; Kay and Legg 1986; Petch 1990; Taylor 1992). This is particularly evident for those leaving an institution to be rehoused in the community, who refer to the sense of satisfaction conveyed by such symbolic markers as being given one's own key, keeping a pet, not having to stay inside, having privacy to see visitors, being able to live with a girlfriend. Furthermore, the implications for someone who has been a long-stay hospital patient of learning to cook, shop and clean should not be underestimated. 'Believing in one's own usefulness matters almost as much to them as being independent. It had given them a feeling of self-worth and of belonging, as well as a sense of purpose.' (Booth *et al.* 1990, p.172)

Ideally, where a community care package is at issue, the user should be at the centre of the assessment process, enabled to articulate his or her needs and wants, and allowed to express choice. In practice care managers find it difficult to adhere to these ideals, given inadequate resources, a narrow range of options, and a professional training which suggests that they are in a better position than their client to identify real needs. As Morris (1993) has pointed out, the danger is of encouraging dependence, and fostering the perception of dangerous or defective people who need looking after, and educated towards behaving in conformity with certain normative conventions.

In effect, support is constructed around a set of value judgements which affirms that professionals are dominant and users are subject to control. Those who construct support packages may tacitly define certain people as unable to manage in a socially acceptable way, who need help to provide them with the skills that will enable them to become socially acceptable, or, if they are beyond achieving those skills, seek to compensate for their lack through packaged care. The agenda is therefore driven from the start by what society, mediated by the professionals, requires, not what the individual labelled person would prefer–which is often the right to be different. Support packages are constructed around a type of person rather than an individual, and take a particular view about how that person's needs for accommodation and support might be met: a person with learning disabilities is suited to a group home with supervision and tuition in living skills provided by resident staff; an older person should be placed in sheltered housing with support provided by a warden, and summon emergency help through an alarm cord; a physically disabled person needs adaptations to his/her existing home which will enable him/her to dispense with as much personal care as possible. This tendency towards stereotyping denies the right to self-determination, and the freedom to choose. It may be for example, that an older person might prefer to struggle alone in a much-loved home and retain independence, perceiving a warden and an alarm cord as unnecessary invasions of privacy; a person with learning difficulties may not wish to share a house with others and be constantly supervised by staff; a physically disabled person may welcome the socialisation opportunity afforded by having a personal carer instead of a home filled with machinery.

These examples, and the above discussion of support, demonstrate how inextricably related are the issues of housing and support. Suitable, appropriate housing in which the occupant feels at ease will promote physical, mental and emotional well-being and thus diminish both the objectively defined and subjectively experienced need for support, whilst inadequate, defective housing in which the occupant feels oppressed or unable to cope will render the need for support more likely. A frail elderly woman with arthritis and a heart condition will have very different support needs depending on whether she lives on the fourth floor of a poorly maintained tenement block without a lift, with a coal fire, local shops half a mile away and no family, or whether she is in a centrally heated bungalow, with shops round the corner and a daughter in the next street.

Supported accommodation - a 'homely' setting?

The government White Paper *Caring for People* in a much quoted phrase, states that community care is to enable people 'to live as independently as possible in their own homes, or in "homely" settings in the community' (DoH 1989, para 1.1). In other words it is about ensuring that as few people as possible are placed in the position of having to enter, or stay in, an institution. Although the reality of community care was about cutting the resultant costs of institutional care and achieving better value for public money, much of the rhetoric was in terms of the concept of normalisation; the right to live ordinary lives, in ordinary settings, and be valued members of a community. This is not the place to engage with the debate about normalisation, about which there is an extensive literature (see for example Brown and Smith 1992; Ramon 1991; Tyne 1982). Suffice it to say that there are misconceptions about the term:

> Normalisation has been frequently misunderstood. It implies that the ties and controls long exercised by statutory agencies over individual lives should be loosened, but it is not enough to assume that something better will emerge of its own volition. Some people believed that normalisation was just common sense, treating people as if they had no disabilities or making people 'normal', when in fact the principle is about good quality care in valued settings. (Knapp *et al.* 1992, p.139)

The idea of 'valued settings' follows the ideology of normalisation, and in practice suggests a setting which is acceptable to the individual and society, which is non-stigmatised, and allows the individual to participate in the activities and lifestyle which most take for granted. As such, it goes further than the inward looking concept of a 'homely' setting, with its overtones of cosiness, and looks beyond, towards integration into community life.

The ideal of a valued and homely setting is a home of one's own, but for many this ideal is not achievable, and a short- or long-term solution is found in supported accommodation. Such accommodation is also frequently referred to as 'special needs' accommodation, the specialist housing generally provided by housing associations, which predates the community care legislation, and caters for the needs of those marginalised by mainstream or 'general' needs housing provision (Arnold *et al.* 1993; Clapham and Smith 1990; Watson and Cooper 1992). It is interesting to note that the adoption of the term 'supported accommodation' has increased since the community care legislation. This has the effect of shifting the emphasis towards the support and away from the 'specialness' of the occupants, occupants who may have been allocated such accommodation as a result of a community care assessment process or by other routes. In the main, special needs schemes have been set up to serve a specific client group, for example older people, people with mental health problems, ex-offenders, refugees, HIV or AIDS patients, who are defined as a group having certain support needs which are best catered for in segregated accommodation or special needs schemes.

The range of supported accommodation is extensive, representing a continuum from less to more supervision or intensity of support provision, and includes:

- scatter(ed) flats – self-contained flats dispersed amongst housing stock where someone (for example a caretaker) can keep an eye on the individual, and where back-up support is available

- cluster flats – self-contained flats in a single house, or scattered in a small area amongst general needs housing, with a locally based support team, offering peripatetic support or a centre to which people can go

- adult placement or supported lodgings – a person is placed in a household where one or more members are willing to provide some support

- shared housing – generally on the model of a bedsitter with shared kitchen and bathroom and communal living areas. Staffed during the day with 24 hour on call cover, or resident staff, and providing communal meals and other activities

- staffed hostels – single or shared rooms, staffed 24 hours a day, usually intended to be transitional, non-permanent accommodation whilst awaiting move-on places

- sheltered housing, category 1 – for the active elderly, a group of self-contained bedsits, flats, houses or bungalows with an alarm call service, limited communal facilities (for example a laundry), occasionally a resident warden

- sheltered housing, category 2 – for the less active, self-contained bedsits or flats with a resident warden and more extensive communal facilities and activities

- very sheltered housing/extra care housing, category 2 ½ – self-contained flats or bedsits for the frail elderly requiring more support, for example the provision of meals and some personal care such as helping to get dressed, bathing, but no nursing care

- residential care homes (part three homes) – providing single rooms with communal facilities including meals, full personal care but not medical care, for the elderly or those with disabilities

- nursing homes – providing full personal and medical care in single or shared rooms.

Although the first few categories are attempts to provide more integrated supported accommodation, on the whole these housing options are signified, or stigmatised, by the provision of segregated accommodation where the occupants' lives are monitored by support providers and care assistants, and where the 'ties and controls' by statutory agencies are in effect maintained and perpetuated rather than loosened. Furthermore, the provision of accommodation is tied to the provision of the type of support that is offered in that accommodation, so that needing (or being diagnosed as needing) a particular type of support means moving to the accommodation. Similarly, having a need for a particular type of accommodation means being obliged to accept the support that goes with it, whether this is entirely appropriate or not. It has the added effect that when individuals no longer need the support, or require additional support, they are also in danger of losing the accommodation, or on the other hand, if they wish to leave the accommodation they also lose the support. Research for example on the needs of older people has shown that most move to sheltered housing because their existing accommodation is inadequate, and not because they require or even appreciate the warden or communal facilities (Fennell 1987; Oldman 1990). Subsequently, at the time at which they need extra support as their needs increase, they have to move again as a traditional sheltered scheme cannot provide the necessary services. An additional problem lies in the shortage of suitable 'move-on' accommodation; more self-contained forms of living to which people are intended to move after a period in supported schemes where they learn or re-learn more independent living skills. These factors negate the principles which community care is supposed to promote, of independence, integration, responsibility and choice (Pritlove 1985), and perpetuate the idea that certain groups of people need 'special' care which has to be provided in a 'special' place. Supported accommodation thus frames or even legitimises the dependency referred to by Morris (1993), and the danger is for the restrictions of an institution to be reproduced in the community.

In an extension of Pritlove's (1985) analysis it can be shown that supported accommodation can be re-interpreted as promoting a set of objectives or values, one or more of which will be brought into play according to the circumstances and characteristics of the individuals assigned to that supported accommodation:

- control – maintaining discipline and authority, albeit in a velvet glove, suggesting that the recipient is naughty, stubborn or childlike

- containment – keeping difficult people and problems under restraint and away from others who might be offended

- protection – of the individual from society or of society from the individual, suggestive of violence, danger or contamination

- order – re-establishing order in a life which appears disordered and in danger of disintegrating

- rehabilitation – attempting to enable the sick or disabled to return to the position they were in before an episode of sickness or disability, even though this may not be achievable (Pritlove 1985).

- modification – the transformation of 'unacceptable' to 'acceptable' behaviour, whether by therapeutic or behavioural means

- compensation – to compensate for the independence which cannot be achieved, making up for something which sadly is not possible (Pritlove 1985).

Within institutions these elements were more transparent; within the community their continued but suppressed existence is more dubious.

Supported accommodation is provided by housing associations, voluntary organisations and local authorities. Local authorities concentrate mainly on sheltered housing, but also have some schemes for other client groups, especially for vulnerable young single people and the homeless. The support element may be provided by the organisation which develops and manages the scheme, or otherwise by another agency under a management agreement, or, if it concerns two departments within a local authority, under a service level agreement. Such an agreement sets out the respective responsibilities of each agency and constitutes a legal contract. Agencies providing support include social services departments, health authorities, housing associations and voluntary agencies.

One of the key issues in supported accommodation is that of funding, as a certain amount of 'top-up funding' is generally required on top of the rent that can be charged to the individual for the accommodation itself. This top-up funding covers the support element, and may be made up from one or more sources, including social services, health authorities, charities, or from the capital or income of the user or his or her family. In addition, the need for a more intensive level of housing management in supported accommodation has been recognised by the regulatory bodies for housing associations, the Housing Corporation in England, Tai Cymru in Wales and Scottish Homes in Scotland, who all provide a revenue allowance (respectively Special Needs Management Allowance (SNMA), Special Housing Revenue Grant (SHRG), Special Needs Allowance Package (SNAP), all undergoing review at the time of writing). The functions that are covered by intensive housing management under this definition are for example, information about housing options, explanations about tenancy rights and responsibilities, general advice and information, liaison with other agencies on the tenant's behalf, limited benefits and income maintenance advice, and dispute resolution. These functions, related to the way in which the person as *tenant* copes with the tenancy, can therefore be provided by the managing, as opposed to the support agency, leaving the support agency to deal with those functions related to the person as *client*.

Local authority accommodation does not attract a revenue allowance for intensive housing management, and where a community care package is not provided, recourse may be had to housing benefit to cover service charges for some support elements, although this cannot be paid for personal care. The regulations relating to housing benefit are not tightly defined, allowing variation between local authorities in their interpretation. The use of the housing benefit system for any support element has been questioned by government and, as with the special management allowances referred to above, is currently under review. (See Clapham and Franklin 1994a; Clapham *et al.* 1994; Griffiths 1997 for more discussion of these issues).

'In their own homes' – who supports?

The majority of people in need of support are likely to be housed in independent self-contained housing in the community, whether this is owner occupied, or rented. Those in the private sector face an uphill struggle in having their housing and support needs identified and met, unless their needs are brought to the attention of social services departments for a community care assessment. There is a significant lack of a service which can offer advice and information on housing options and the support services available to individuals who are struggling to manage in their own home, with the result that independent living very often means hazardous and isolated living. Agencies which operate to good effect in this field are the Care and Repair or Staying Put schemes. These schemes assist older and disabled people to stay in their own homes by providing advice not only on the feasibility and funding sources of aids, adaptations and renovations but also in regard to the wider needs of the individual for income maintenance advice, social contacts and so on (Harrison and Means 1990; Leather and Mackintosh 1992). Care and Repair has been especially effective in Wales, where all but two local authorities are covered by such agencies. In England access to schemes is more limited, although the necessity for more comprehensive coverage is acknowledged.

It is now accepted almost as a *cliché* that local authority housing has become the housing of last resort; a residualised sector occupied by those with no other choice, and who are marginalised in the housing market. By definition therefore, local authorities are providing for a sector of the population which is disadvantaged, whether through poverty, general vulnerability, old age, ill- health, or more serious disability. Evidence suggests that housing associations, as they take over the provider role from what is now constituted as the enabling local authority, are increasingly facing similar problems in their general needs housing stock (Burrows 1997; Page 1993). What both sectors are therefore facing is an increasingly dependent population, whose ability to cope is compromised, and who therefore have actual or potential support needs. Some of these people will be receiving support services through a community care package, but the majority will not.

It is very often the staff of the housing organisation, through the contact brought about by managing the property, who first become aware of a problem. This may be at the point at which they are allocating a property to a new tenant, or may arise during the course of a tenancy. The question then for housing organisations is what, if anything, they should do about it. The logical course of action is to alert the local social services department, in the hope that it will be able to assist the person concerned. Sometimes this is successful, but frequently social workers will respond by saying that the case is not serious enough, that they have limited resources, and that they have to concentrate on certain priority groups, such as children and older people (Clapham and Franklin 1994a; Franklin and Clapham 1997). Housing organisations are then put in the position of having to deal with the situation, or ignoring it until crisis point is reached.

This whole issue raises the question as to the rightful role of housing management, and whether it should be providing a social and welfare role, as opposed to only a 'bricks and mortar' or property management service. Over the course of its history as a separate profession, starting in the late nineteenth century, there has never been any adequate and clear definition of housing management as an area of work. Depending on the characteristics of the tenants housed, the emphasis has fluctuated between a concentration on administrative functions (such as rent collection, repairs monitoring, the letting of properties) and a concern to improve the social and moral condition of tenants. These issues have come to the fore in the policy context of the 1990s, due to the implementation of community care, the debate about revenue funding (whether through the Housing Revenue Account, Housing Benefit, or special management allowances), the move towards the more commercial management of housing as evidenced by value-for-money targets and performance indicators, and the need to specify for compulsory competitive tendering (Clapham and Franklin 1994b).

The Chartered Institute of Housing, the umbrella organisation of housing services, has argued quite strongly for the adoption of a social and welfare role, given the increasingly vulnerable nature of the tenants housed, and has lobbied government to this effect (IoH 1993). That this has been reluctantly accepted, at least by the Department of the Environment, is demonstrated in a circular which suggests that where necessary, and at the discretion of the local authority concerned, welfare services may be provided by housing management staff in local authority departments, and may even be a significant part of their job (DoE 1995). Such welfare services include counselling and support in connection with tenants' well-being, health and personal needs, organising social and leisure activities, liaising with health and social services, but exclude activities defined as personal care such as assistance with washing, feeding, or nursing.

Research has confirmed that housing organisations, both local authority housing departments and housing associations, have been carrying out these functions for some time, and recently to an increasing extent (Clapham and Franklin 1994a; Franklin and Clapham 1997; Gregory and Brownill 1995). There is enormous variation between local authorities and housing associations in the extent to which they perceive the need to carry out a support role. Some consider that it is categorically not within their terms of reference, not least because once they have started they will find it difficult to 'draw the line'. Such authorities may well refuse to take on any tenant who they suspect may have support needs unless there is an agreement or contract with a support agency, and will use lack of requisite support as a justification for eviction. In others, housing officers feel themselves drawn into providing a support role either by default, because there is no other agency willing or able to do so, or because they actually wish to provide that support themselves. The justification is that by so doing they are enabling the tenant to sustain the tenancy, and in the longer term this is helping to fulfil their primary aim of property management. In some cases specialist workers are employed, for example tenancy support workers, family support workers, resettlement workers, case workers, wardens, or concierges, whose specific job remit is to provide support. In other cases generic housing officers provide a support role as part of their wider job remit. For many it is this aspect of the job which provides interest, variety and challenge, and offers a more personal involvement with tenants. Some, more especially the specialist workers, perceive their role as being very similar to that of a social worker, and that they have the same sort of case work approach (Clapham and Franklin 1994a; Franklin and Clapham 1997).

Support in these terms is often directed towards the early stages of a tenancy, ensuring that a tenant chooses or is allocated a suitable property, has furniture, knows which benefits can be claimed, possesses reasonable daily living skills, is aware of local community facilities and is encouraged to participate in them. Support directed towards an existing tenant may involve a housing officer befriending a tenant and making sure he or she is visited regularly, discussing alternative housing options, endeavouring to resolve a difficult situation with neighbours, making sure the grass is cut, and that rubbish is removed. In more challenging cases it may involve crisis management such as dealing with attempted suicide, with physical abuse, self-neglect, infestations or criminal activity. In some instances it will involve drawing in other agencies to help the tenant, such as medical services, the police, environmental health, or home care, but after these services have withdrawn it becomes an issue of keeping an eye on the tenant to ensure the same crisis does not recur.

The involvement of housing agencies in support, however, is by necessity of a limited nature, and the sad truth is that those living independently in the community are not getting the level of support that they or their carers need. For example, the Office of Population Census and Surveys investigation into people aged over 65 reported that one in eight of those interviewed who needed support had none (OPCS 1994), whilst the DoE report *Living Independently* showed that of the four-fifths of their sample of 9000 older and disabled people who wished to remain at home, three-quarters needed more help (McCafferty 1994). As the budgets of the caring services, whether under the heading of community care, health or nursing care, or the support provided by voluntary agencies, become ever more constrained, the numbers of those receiving adequate, or indeed any, help diminishes. In this way, the very rhetoric of community care, about independent living, becomes a mockery, since those who stand to benefit are those who will be forced out of their homes because of the lack of support. The issue becomes one that is the opposite of that found in supported accommodation, with its danger of perpetuating dependency and the recreation of institutions in the community, to one of floundering in a situation of unsupported desolation, without framework or direction. It is no longer then a case of trying to stitch together the edges of the seam, but of trying to avoid falling into the gaping hole of neglect.

Towards seamless solutions?

Growing dissatisfaction with the concept of special needs accommodation, in conjunction with the recognition that what is often needed in independent living is not so much professional social work input as help in ordinary living skills and coping strategies, is beginning to promote new ways of thinking about the provision of support. New mechanisms are being devised, particularly by housing associations, to enable support to be delivered to people so that they can remain in their own homes, or move into independent accommodation for the first time.

Floating support

One such mechanism, which is becoming more popular, is that of floating support. The narrow definition of floating support (Morris 1995) is tied to the funding regimes of the Housing Corporation, Tai Cymru and Scottish Homes referred to above. This revenue allowance, previously linked to particular schemes of supported accommodation, has been extended to cover intensive housing management provided in self-contained accommodation. The principle is to enable people to receive the support they need to maintain independent accommodation and to help them to sustain their tenancies. The intention is that this support will be of short-term duration, and that when it ceases, it allows another tenant who needs similar assistance to receive that same support.

The broader definition of floating support (Morris 1995) covers not only the above additional housing management tasks, funded by special allowances, but a wider range of functions, funded generally from other charitable or statutory grants. This allows more intensive packages of support to be provided, for a longer duration. At present these floating support schemes are usually conceived and delivered separately from the community care process, but clearly have a key role to play within it. Housing associations use floating support in a variety of ways: to support people moving into general needs accommodation from an institution, from a position of homelessness, or from temporary accommodation; as an alternative to special needs schemes; and for those already in general needs accommodation who develop support needs. The advantage of floating support, particularly in its broader definition, is that it breaks the tie between accommodation and support, and makes it possible to devise a programme of support which is tailor made to individuals, thus putting user need at the centre of the process. In many instances a care plan is drawn up in discussion with the individual, which sets out specific areas in which support is needed, including social and personal care, but rarely medical care other than checking that medication is taken, and with a staged progression to complete independence where possible. Other statutory or voluntary services are drawn in as required.

Clearly, the main benefit of floating support is its flexibility; the fact that it can be 'floated' in or out of a mainstream tenancy as and when and to the extent that it is needed, without in any way jeopardising the right of the recipient to remain in the property. However, as Morris (1995) has noted there are a number of issues which still need to be resolved, amongst them the unsatisfactory funding mechanisms, the boundaries between intensive housing management and floating support, and between floating support and the responsibilities of other caring services.

Links to the community

A number of housing associations are beginning to see the benefits of extending the services they offer in supported accommodation to those in the surrounding community. The leader in this field has been Anchor Housing Association, whose main role is to provide sheltered and extra care housing for older people. They have piloted the concept of outreach care teams attached to schemes, who offer home care to older people thus enabling them to remain in their own homes. They also make the facilities of the scheme itself available to people in the community, for example lunch clubs, hairdressing, chiropody, financial advice and bathing for people with physical disabilities (Rawson 1990). Other housing associations are also moving into outreach services to enable a variety of client groups to stay in their own homes who might otherwise be at risk (Belcher 1995).

These developments are certainly a step forward in enabling independent living, but are generally undertaken in response to the need of housing associations to diversify in the light of uncertain development and revenue funding situations. Furthermore, they still rely to a large extent on partnership with health and social service authorities, with the potential for the gaps in services already noted. However, as Belcher suggests in his article, housing associations are well equipped to take on a wider role, and make sure that community care can work:

> Their experience with vulnerable client groups and their ethos of individual
> rights, based on tenancy agreements, gives them vital tools to do the

job...Housing associations have a chance, and perhaps a duty, to make a crucial contribution. (Belcher 1995, p.14)

Conclusion

This chapter has endeavoured to show the essential nature of the links between housing and support, and that for those people who are vulnerable through sickness, age or disability, the one crucially impacts on the other. In effect the two are inseparable; limitations in support affect the suitability of the home, and limitations of the home affect the need for support. Furthermore, a house is not simply a physical structure, with its influence confined to such matters as accessibility, location and adaptability (although these are vitally important), it is also a place to feel at ease, a place of memories, a place of security and control, a centre of activities (Després 1991); a place in which the self-actualising process is most fully achieved. Having to move away from home often displaces a part of one's identity, and can initiate a process of bereavement for which no amount of support can compensate. Similarly, moving into a home for the first time is symbolic of emergence into a new identity, away from the boundaries and denial of self-determination found in an institution. Supported accommodation may provide a valuable half-way house, but that is all it can ever hope to be; a middle way between independence and dependence, but always erring towards dependence. The new models of support currently being developed offer an alternative which is person-centred, and which fits more closely with the aims of care in the community.

Housing organisations and support providers should be charged with the duty to assess the limitations and opportunities of the available housing and support together, rather than in isolation, and to examine how the service each provides can act to enhance or detract from the service or facilities provided by the other. In this process the user should be respected as an individual with individual needs, and enabled to make an informed choice, rather than being dogmatically steered in one direction or another according to the agendas of the service providers. Unfortunately it is rare for housing providers to consider their tenants as individual users of services, just as it is rare for support providers to understand the constraints under which housing providers operate. Both appear to have a limited view of the complexities of the meaning of house as home, and of the need to shake off the preconceptions which inhibit a more holistic approach to the assessment of need and appraisal of solutions (Franklin 1996). What is required ideally is a supportive environment, in which housing and support complement each other to provide the maximum freedom with which the individuals concerned feel they can cope.

References

Allen, C., Clapham, D. and Franklin, B. (1995) *The Future of Care in the Community.* Edinburgh: Scottish Homes.

Anderson, I. (1994) *Access to Housing for Low Income Single People.* York: Centre for Housing Policy.

Arblaster, L., Conway, J., Foreman, A. and Hawtin, M. (1996) *Asking the Impossible? Inter-Agency Working to Address the Housing, Health and Social Care Needs of People in Ordinary Housing.* Bristol: Policy Press.

Arnold, P., Bochel, H., Broadhurst, S. and Page, D. (1993) *Community Care: The Housing Dimension.* York: Joseph Rowntree Foundation.

Belcher, J. (1995) 'Housing Associations and Community Care.' *Housing and Planning Review 50,* 2, 13–15.

Booth, T., Simons, K. and Booth, W. (1990) *Outward Bound: Relocation and Community Care for People with Learning Difficulties.* Buckingham: Open University Press.

Brown, H. and Smith, H. (eds) (1992) *Normalisation: A Reader for the Nineties.* London: Routledge.

Burrows, R. (1997) *Contemporary Patterns of Residential Mobility in Relation to Social Housing in England.* York: Centre for Housing Policy.

Clapham, D. and Franklin, B. (1994a) *The Housing Management Contribution to Community Care.* Glasgow: Centre for Housing Research and Urban Studies.

Clapham, D. and Franklin, B. (1994b) *Housing Management, Community Care and Competitive Tendering.* Coventry: Chartered Institute of Housing.

Clapham, D. and Smith, S. (1990) 'Housing policy and "special needs".' *Policy and Politics 18,* 3, 193–205.

Clapham, D., Munro, M. and Kay, H. (1994) *A Wider Choice: Revenue Funding Mechanisms for Housing and Community Care.* York: Joseph Rowntree Foundation.

Dalley, G. (1988) *Ideologies of Caring: Rethinking Community and Collectivism.* London: Macmillan.

Department of the Environment (1995) *The Housing Revenue Account.* Circular 8/95. London: DoE.

Department of Health (1989) *Caring for People: Community Care in the Next Decade and Beyond.* London: HMSO.

Department of Health (1993) *Integrating the Housing Agenda into Community Care.* London: Department of Health, Community Care Support Force.

Després, C. (1991) 'The meaning of home: Literature review and directions for future research and theoretical development.' *Journal of Architectural and Planning Research 8,* 2, 96–115.

Fennell, G. (1987) *A Place of My Own: A Consumer View of Very Sheltered Housing in Scotland.* Edinburgh: Bield Housing Association.

Franklin, B. (1996) 'New perspectives on housing and support for older people.' In R. Bland (ed) *Developing Services for Older People and Their Families.* London: Jessica Kingsley Publishers.

Franklin, B. (forthcoming) 'More than community care: Supporting the transition from homelessness to home.' In S. Hutson and D. Clapham (eds) *Homelessness: Public Policies and Private Troubles.* London: Cassell.

Franklin, B. and Clapham, D. (1997) 'The social construction of housing management.' *Housing Studies 12,* 1, 7–26.

Gregory, S. and Brownill, S. (1995) *The Housing/Care Divide: Community Care and the Management of Single Person Housing in Oxford.* Oxford: Oxford Brookes University.

Griffiths, R. (1988) *Community Care: Agenda for Action.* London: HMSO.

Griffiths, S. (1997) *Housing Benefit and Supported Housing: The Impact of Recent Changes.* York: York Publishing Services.

Gulstad, J. (1987) *The Right to be Ordinary: A Study of Obstacles and Achievements in Community Care in Scotland.* Glasgow: Glasgow Special Housing Group.

Harrison, L. and Means, R. (1990) *Housing: The Essential Element in Community Care.* Oxford: Anchor.

House of Commons Social Services Committee (1990) *Community Care: Services for People with a Mental Handicap and People with a Mental Illness.* London: HMSO.

Institute of Housing (1993) *Housing Welfare Services and the Housing Revenue Account.* Coventry: IoH.

Kay, A. and Legg, C. (1986) *Discharged to the Community: A Review of Housing and Support in London for People Leaving Psychiatric Care.* London: Good Practice in Mental Health.

Knapp, M., Cambridge, P., Thomson, C., Beecham, J., Allen, C. and Darton, R. (1992) *Care in the Community: Challenge and Demonstration.* Aldershot: Ashgate.

Leather, P. and Mackintosh, S. (1992) *Maintaining Home Ownership: The Agency Approach.* London: IoH/Longman.

Lund, B. and Foord, M. (1997) *Towards Integrated Living? Housing Strategies and Community Care.* Bristol: The Policy Press.

McCafferty, P. (1994) *Living Independently: A Study of the Housing Needs of Elderly and Disabled People.* London: HMSO.

Means, R. and Smith, R. (1994) *Community Care: Policy and Practice.* London: Macmillan.

Morris, J. (1989) *Able Lives: Women's Experience of Paralysis.* London: Women's Press.

Morris, J. (1993) *Community Care or Independent Living.* York: Joseph Rowntree Trust.

Morris, J. (1995) *Housing and Floating Support: A Review.* York: York Publishing Services.

National Federation of Housing Associations (1992) *Assessment of the Housing Requirements of People with Special Needs over the Next Decade.* London: NFHA.

Oldman, C. (1990) *Moving in Old Age: New Directions in Housing Policies.* London: HMSO.

Office of Population Census and Surveys (1994) *People Aged 65 and Over.* London: HMSO.

Page, D. (1993) *Building for Communities: A Study of New Housing Association Estates.* York: Joseph Rowntree Foundation.

Petch, A. (1990) *Heaven Compared to a Hospital Ward.* Stirling: Social Work Research Centre, Stirling University.

Pleace, N. (1995) *Housing Single Vulnerable People*. York: Centre for Housing Policy.

Pritlove, J. (1985) *Group Homes: An Inside Story*. Sheffield: Joint Unit for Social Services Research.

Ramon, S. (ed) (1991) *Beyond Community Care: Normalisation and Integration Work*. London: Macmillan.

Rawson, D. (1990) *Commercial Enterprises and Sheltered Housing*. Oxford: Anchor Housing Association.

Spicker, P. (1993) *Housing and Community Care in Scotland*. Glasgow: Shelter Scotland.

Taylor, I. (1992) *Discharged with Care: A Report on Practical Arrangements for People Leaving Psychiatric Hospital and the Prevention of Homelessness*. Edinburgh: Scottish Council for Single Homelessness.

Tyne, A. (1982) 'Community care and mentally handicapped people.' In A. Walker (ed) *Community Care*. Oxford: Blackwell.

Ungerson, C. (1987) *Policy is Personal*. London: Tavistock.

Villeneau, L. (1992) *Housing with Care and Support: A Quality Action Guide*. London: MIND.

Watson, L. (1996) *Housing Need and Community Care: The Housing Pathway Pilot Programme*. London: NFHA/CIH.

Watson, L. and Conway, T. (1995) *Homes for Independent Living: Housing and Community Care Strategies*. Coventry: Chartered Institute of Housing.

Watson, L. and Cooper, R. (1992) *Housing with Care: Supported Housing and Housing Associations*. York: Joseph Rowntree Foundation.

CHAPTER 10

From Benign Neglect to Malign Indifference?
Housing and Young People

Mark Drakeford and Howard Williamson

The 'terms of trade' in the relationship between young people and the wider society have altered dramatically in recent years, largely adversely for the young (Carnegie United Kingdom Trust 1997). Youth transitions to adulthood and to full 'citizenship' have become more extended, more precarious and more complex (see for example Morrow and Richards 1966). Indeed, this has led to some significant paradigm shifts in theoretical formulations of transition. A focus on economic transitions and the trajectories from education to the labour market shaped significantly by differentiated structural forces (class, race, gender and geography) has been supplanted by a more eclectic focus on social, psychological and economic transitions determined unpredictably by rapidly changing structural forces and by the capacity of young people to maximise their own possibilities through effective 'life management' (Helve and Bynner 1996). The old certainties around work, family and housing transitions have been fractured, and routes to adulthood have been depicted as akin to 'snakes and ladders' (Coles 1995). Young people have to negotiate or navigate different pathways from dependency to independence. The life course is more fluid and more subject to personal decision-making, although the old 'grand narratives' which shaped young people's futures in the past have by no means disappeared. Young people have different resources at their disposal, according to their class and family backgrounds, which affect the 'choices' they will make. Nonetheless, there are still choices—in transitions from school to the labour market, from families of origin to families of destination, and from dependent to independent living (Jones and Wallace 1992). However, some of these choices are heavily constrained; more disadvantaged young people are likely to face particular difficulties in minimising risk and maximising possibility. They will make false starts and sideways moves, which are more likely to produce marginalisation than inclusion. In this way, transitions become 'fractured' rather than developmental.

Youth policy in the United Kingdom has not assisted young people coping with these prolonged transitions. In domains from education and training to criminal justice the consequence of changing legislation and policy has been to worsen the position of already disadvantaged young people (Williamson 1993). Those denied constructive institutional support are often also young people who are unable to draw on family support (such as young people in care), and, as a result, who face greater disruption in all aspects of transition (Morrow and Richards 1996) and are more at risk of homelessness, unemployment, crime, and drug misuse. It is the first of these risks which this chapter is concerned with, and the role that social work may play in alleviating and ameliorating the circumstances of those threatened with, or actually experiencing homelessness.

In considering youth homelessness, we have endeavoured to combine both a wide and narrow focus. It is imperative that any discussion is located firmly within the broader context of the housing needs of young people. Homelessness lies at the most acute end of a spectrum which encompasses a complex pattern of need and supply through which young people attempt to negotiate their transition from dependent to independent accommodation. While this chapter will concentrate—as has most research – on the effect of homelessness, it cannot properly be understood without some reference to the wider factors which help prevent homelessness from taking place, or which propel young people in that direction. Indeed, as we will note in more detail below, successful housing transitions are invariably the product of an invisible raft of supportive mechanisms, particularly emotional and material assistance from family networks (Ainley 1991; Jones 1995), yet it is this that is often lacking for those young people who require it most urgently, namely those who are accelerated into the independent housing market as a result of difficult family circumstances – those who are at high risk of becoming homeless. In short, those young people who need most support are least likely to have access to it. It is a circular argument, but one which is central to understanding the context within which youth homelessness will emerge. It is an argument which is often overlooked in the considerable literature which now exists on youth homelessness. This literature is important because it draws attention to the 'invisible' dimensions of homelessness (sleeping on friends' floors, in disused caravans and bus shelters, for example) and forges necessary connections to the wider tangle of pathologies experienced by young people, such as poor health and criminality. However, it rarely addresses either the broader housing policy context (though see Hutson and Liddiard 1994) nor the support which may be forthcoming from social services (though see McCluskey 1994), about which this chapter is concerned.

In considering social work, we make a similar observation. In theory, social workers might assume responsibility for assisting any young person who comes to a local authority or voluntary project seeking help with a housing need. In practice, the focus is far narrower. Social work interventions concentrate on troubled and troublesome young people who, for the purposes of this chapter, are 'dealt with' in three distinct ways. First, social workers support and shore up family arrangements which have become strained or are under threat of breakdown. Second, they work with young people, and often their families, where those young people are voluntarily or compulsorily living in residential settings such as local authority accommodation, custody, a psychiatric unit or a residential school. Third, they work with young people who have moved to live in a range of independent settings along a continuum from staffed and supported residential units to full tenancies in public or private rented accommodation. Social work practice with young people at risk of, or experiencing, homelessness is therefore also detached from its wider context, and recognition of its broader possibilities in relation to youth homelessness is the purpose of this chapter.

This chapter therefore explores the work which social welfare organisations undertake with young people at the most acute end of housing need. In doing so, it necessarily considers some of the more general principles and practice of social work with young people, in order to assess the ways they help or hinder those facing or experiencing the most extreme and abject housing plight.

Social welfare and young people: The extent of contact

Social workers come into contact with young people in a wide variety of contexts, most of which, in contemporary practice, are characterised by crisis of one sort or another. An important debate continues to take place within the profession concerning the balance between reactive and preventative services (see for example, Colton, Drury and Williams 1995 for an account of these arguments within the child care sphere). The last 15 years have, however, witnessed a shift–across the board of social welfare services for young people–away from the sort of work which, arguably, might prevent problems such as homelessness, and towards dealing with such difficulties only when they have taken place, and when informal networks of family and friends have proved inadequate in rendering assistance. This shift has taken place at a time when a number of other developments have formed core characteristics of social work in this area.

First, across the board of service provision, social workers come into contact with large numbers of young people at times of transition and such individuals make up a substantial proportion of their total caseloads. Second, significant numbers of these young people are in accommodation circumstances at the acute end of the need spectrum, often removed against their consent from homes and families and almost always facing volatile or uncertain accommodation futures. From the perspective of any one individual, of course, involvement with social welfare workers may encompass all three services considered here, and others. As Connelly and Crown (1994) suggest,

> Single homeless people have a higher risk of death and disease than comparable housed people. Excess deaths are due mainly to suicide, accidents and violence, and alcohol-related and respiratory diseases...Single homeless people are more likely to have serious mental illness than the general population. Schizophrenia is the most commonly diagnosed disorder. (pp.xv/xvi)

A few facts and figures about the scale and nature of social work practice with young people serve to illustrate these arguments. In child and family social work, 29 per cent of the 34,900 names on Child Protection Registers in England and Wales on 31st Mach 1994 belonged to individuals of more than 10 years of age (Department of Health 1995; Welsh Office 1995). Outcomes within the system of family support services are most acute when they lead to children being 'looked after' by a local authority, rather than their parents. There are currently some 52,000 children in Wales and England in such circumstances, including both those who are accommodated by voluntary agreement with parents and those who are the subject of a care order (NCH 1995, p.111). On breaking these figures down by age, once again, a pattern emerges in which these most intrusive interventions are concentrated upon older young people. Of those children looked after in the year to 31st March 1994, 42 per cent were aged between 10 and 15, 20 per cent aged 16 and 17 and a further 1 per cent aged beyond 17 (Department of Health 1994).

While such figures emphasise the scale of work undertaken by child and family social workers, they give little indication of the quality of resources, or of the ways in which access to such provision may be obtained. Recent research in South Wales suggests that the Act's intention that 'appropriate accommodation' should be made available when necessary remains the single greatest area of difficulty for practitioners. Problems were identified in terms both of range of alternative resources and adequacy of supply. Access was restricted to those children and young people where need was acute and overwhelming and then on the basis of what happened to be available rather than any assessment of particular requirements.

Resource starvation and instability are equally acute phenomena of youth justice practice. Accommodation issues in this sphere are concentrated around those points in the Court process which can result in young people being removed from home. These occur at both pre-trial stages (when questions of bail and remand arise) and at sentence, when custodial sentencing may occur. The pattern of youth justice contact shifted radically during the 1980s as principles of maximum diversion and minimum intervention came to shape practice actions. The proportion of known indictable offences committed by those aged 10-16 dealt with by means of a caution, for example, rose from 50 per cent in 1979 to more than 80 per cent by 1992 (Home Office 1993). At each point in the criminal justice process, however, from arrest to final sentence and beyond, the availability or otherwise of suitable and stable accommodation has an impact upon decisions made (see Haines and Drakeford 1997 for further details). Accommodation circumstances viewed favourably by the Courts contribute to less intrusive criminal justice outcomes. Those young people already disadvantaged by problems in their living arrangements (and especially those in local authority accommodation, see Collins and Kelly 1995) find that these difficulties compound the problems they face in the criminal justice arena.

Finally, in this brief review, it is useful to consider the involvement of young people within the psychiatric services. According to Wilson (1995) most prevalence figures now indicate that around 20% of all children have some kind of mental health problem. This amounts to approximately two million children under the age of 16 in England and Wales. About two per cent, that is about 40,000 children, have mental health problems that are severe enough as to be seriously disabling problems which are persistent, extreme in the ways in which they present themselves, and which cause great distress to the young   people themselves and to their families. (p.62)

A rapid growth in the number of young people undergoing residential psychiatric treatment has been a defining characteristic of work in this area. Between 1986 and 1992, for example, admissions per thousand of the population rose by 50 per cent for those under the age of 10, by 24 per cent for young people aged between 10 and 14 and by 11 per cent for those aged between 15 and 19. These figures are all the more startling when compared to a decline in proportionate admissions of 11 per cent for those aged between 20 and 74 (NCH 1995, p.61).

Social welfare and young people: Practice principles

Social workers and other social welfare practitioners, therefore, come into contact with large numbers of young people whose circumstances have often become crisis-ridden and are at the sharp end of accommodation need. Increasingly, however, it is only individuals who are in such dire circumstances who are likely to be offered any sort of service. As suggested above, this is partly explained by the resource restrictions which, for more than 15 years, have cumulatively and increasingly faced the major providers of personal social services – the local authorities. The issue is not, however, exclusively to do with a shortage of resources. Within social work itself, a powerful set of practice principles came to be developed over the same period which, from a very different basis, also contributed to a withdrawal of contact from young people whose circumstances were characterised by difficulty, rather than crisis. Put very briefly, the 1969 Children and Young Persons Act encouraged social workers to take a broad view of their remit. In its widest application, it sanctioned the provision of services to any child or young person for whom investment in counteracting disadvantage or difficulty might contribute to the avoidance of greater problems in the future. It was an Act imbued with a positive belief in the possibilities of improvement. The Act was never fully implemented, since its enactment coincided with the advent of a new (Conservative) government with a very different approach to young people, both the troubled and troublesome. Yet social workers enthusiastically embraced those new 'preventative' powers and possibilities which became available under the Act. It all went horribly wrong. Within a decade, in a profoundly influential analysis, Thorpe and colleagues (1980) concluded that the 1969 arrangements had not substituted for the previous system, but had come to run alongside it, sucking into formal contact with social welfare agencies a whole new raft of young people who then found themselves at risk of harsher treatment. These findings, together with the injunctions of American criminologists to 'Leave the Kids Alone' (Schur 1971), combined to produce new approaches to practice in which the avoidance of harm, rather than the promotion of best interests, came to be the first principle of intervention. 'Best interests' became a weasel term, reflecting unscientific professional preferences and assertions rather than any 'objective' benefit to the individual (see Kittrie 1971). Entanglement with a social welfare agency, it was argued, was more likely to lead to increased difficulty for young people – because of, for example, labelling, deviancy amplification, contamination through contact with others, and extended containment and control which was often disproportionate to the initial rationale for intervention. The 'new orthodoxy', as it came to be known (see Jones 1984) suggested that most young people indulged in deviant behaviour and experienced some level of family conflict; this was a normal and inevitable part of growing up. Left to themselves, these difficulties would almost always resolve themselves. Social welfare workers would therefore render the best service by maximising the extent to which such 'normal' courses of action could be allowed to run their course, and minimising the extent to which intervention by formal agencies – however well motivated – should be substituted for them.

Three practice principles came to be regarded as embodying the new approach: maximum diversion, in which young people coming to the attention of social welfare agencies were diverted from formal systems as far as possible; minimum intervention, in which those young people who could not be so diverted were engaged with formal systems only to the minimum possible extent; and systems management, in which the 'career' of those young people drawn more substantially into contact with official organisations was to be influenced, not by attempting to alter the behaviour of young people themselves, but by impacting upon the way that decisions about such young people were made by others.

It is not an argument of this chapter that the ways of working outlined above were not appropriate at the time. Indeed, they were perhaps timely in order to vitiate some of the excesses of state intervention. But they were conceived at a time when opportunities for all young people, in terms of employment, housing, and state benefits, were considerably better than they are today. Leaving the kids alone left the vast majority likely to find a place in the labour market and, with sufficient economic resources, to make the expected transitions to responsible adult life. In contrast, we suggest that the changing social and economic context faced by young people renders such assumptions and non-intervention considerably more problematic: social work practice, and the ideas which inform it, needs retuning in order to respond more appropriately to the changing climate of transition. For many young people, the path to adulthood has become one in which the previous props of employment, family resources and access to independent accommodation, for example, are far less readily available. In these circumstances, to rely on the 'normal' processes of personal and social maturation, and a presumption that sooner or later young people will 'slot in' to adult roles and responsibilities, risks turning a strategy of benign neglect to one of malign indifference. When youth justice workers, for example, confine themselves narrowly to 'confronting offending behaviour', rather than addressing the circumstances in which young people are made vulnerable to offending – arguing that these are somehow subsidiary 'welfare' matters – then two contradictory results are likely to follow. Positively, young people appearing before the Courts will not find themselves drawn into receiving assistance as the dangerous price of having that delivered through a criminal justice sanction, such as a supervision order. Negatively, however, the individual diverted away from punishment may find her or himself without any help at all. Denied assistance by the youth justice arm of social welfare – because they do not present a 'justice' difficulty – some of the most needy young people find themselves unable to obtain attention of any sort.

In some parts of contemporary social commentary, family life and individual responsibility are presented as prey to social workers, intrusively invading personal domains where they are neither welcome nor perceived as helpful. In our experience, the exact opposite far more often appertains. In writing Reports for the Youth Court, for example, the message from parents time and again is one of having sought – and been refused – help from Social Services Departments overwhelmed by the demands of child protection work and with no spare capacity to assist those families whose own resources in assisting adolescents are stretched to breaking point.

In these circumstances what is demanded is a *reconnection* of social workers with the *social* circumstances of their users. These demands are particularly acute in the housing context where absence of sufficient and suitable accommodation for young people continues to be one of the most pressing and recurrent themes in daily practice.

Social welfare and young people: Focus on housing

In the consideration which follows, discussion will largely be confined to the duties which social workers undertake in relation to 16 and 17 year olds. Before moving to do so, however, it is worth recalling that once young homeless people attain the age of 18 even the inadequate protections with which this chapter is mostly concerned fall away. Anderson and Morgan (1997), in their review of local authority and housing association policies and practices, found that 'for young people aged 18–24 the chances of being accepted as vulnerable on the basis of age alone or because of a care background declined significantly.' Leigh (1994) conducted an enquiry into the operation of new community care arrangements in respect of single people. His report concluded that:

> young homeless people under 25 and on reduced benefit entitlements were a major concern to all local authorities...at the age of 18, young homeless people who are not being 'looked after' by the local authority are passed over to adult services under the Community Care Act, which neither considers them   potentially vulnerable, nor provides them with eligibility for the accommodation they need. (p.23)

We have noted already that the period of transition between childhood and adulthood has become extended for young people, and fractured for others as the result of changes in social policy towards them. A proper understanding of the accommodation circumstances faced by young people can only be obtained by placing this within the context of the general rationales advanced to justify such policy development. The redefining of 18 to 24 year olds as a new and subordinate category of citizen lies at the root of the discriminatory way in which such individuals are treated in the accommodation context. Their situation should always be less eligible than the circumstances of anyone prepared to remain within the parental home, however exploitative or socially damaging. As to 16 and 17 year olds, just as they had been held to blame for their own unemployment – and therefore denied benefit by the 1988 Social Security changes – so, within the dominant social policy paradigms of the last fifteen years, their homelessness was also portrayed as largely a matter of choice. Kay (1994) quotes Prime Minister Thatcher in June 1988:

> There are a number of young people who choose voluntarily to leave home. I do not think we can be expected, no matter how many they are, to provide units for them...these young people already have a home to live in, belonging to their parents. (p.5)

Of course, Mrs Thatcher's assertion that young people were able to remain unproblematically at home both wilfully misunderstood the real situation faced in some households and neglected the policy pressures which her government had produced in order to make other courses of action more difficult. Specifically within the accommodation field Housing Benefit for young people has become a favourite target for cuts within the social security budget. In 1996 a general move to restrict the scope of Housing Benefit entitlement included a series of particular reductions for those aged under 25, further narrowing the type of accommodation for which full benefit can be claimed, placing a new low ceiling on eligible rents and confining delivery of benefit to payment in arrears.

    In our introduction we placed the move from family of origin to family of destination within a more general framework of transitions which young people make during the years between childhood and adulthood. Writing specifically of the housing field, Gill Jones (1995) suggests, 'now, in the mid1990s, there is more talk about preventing young people from leaving home than celebrating a major event in the transition to adulthood. Leaving home is seen as inherently problematic' (p.1). Even for well-supported and relatively prosperous young people, she demonstrates that leaving home is more of a process than a simple end in itself. Help with material goods – old carpets, passed-on refrigerators and so on; continued use of services at home – using the washing machine; and a bolt hole in times of difficulty or distress all bolster the chances of successfully making such a transition.

The young people with whom social workers come into contact often stand at the opposite end of the spectrum from those able to draw upon such sustained and reasonably-resourced networks of support. Rather, as Kay (1994) has suggested,

> The fact that the majority of homeless 16 and 17 year olds do not leave home on a whim has been well documented...Care leavers and young people who have left the parental home due to violence, abuse, and eviction are over-represented amongst this age group (Strathdee 1992) [and]...leave home to escape intolerable circumstances, for example physical or sexual abuse. Others are forced to leave as a result of family disputes, often associated with a step-parent. (p.6)

For this group of young people, already vulnerable to 'failure' in housing transitions because of limited support, no 'bolt hole' is available; there is no way back. (CHAR 1996)

A wealth of empirical and research material exists concerning the situation of homeless young people and it is to this evidence which we now turn. As an opening caveat it is worth drawing attention to the warnings provided by a series of writers (McCluskey 1993; Strathdee 1993, for example) concerning the difficulty of gaining accurate statistics on the numbers of homeless 16 and 17 year olds and the particular methodological obstacles which face any researcher studying single homelessness, an issue which is well set out in Hutson and Liddiard (1994). While the particularities may be evasive, however, the well-established general pattern is of a growth in numbers, exemplified dramatically in the late 1980s following 1988 Social Security changes. For some time, there has been a general consensus amongst those agencies dealing with the homeless and charities dealing with young people that around 150,000 young people under the age of 25 experience homelessness each year (Pollitt, Booth and Kay 1989). Of course, the definition of homelessness is contentious. Advocacy groups are likely to favour broad formulations while there is a pronounced political tendency to conceive it in the narrowest terms. We favour the definition adopted by Davies *et al.* (1996) which was originated by Hutson and Liddiard (1994): that is 'not being in or having immediate or easy access to secure accommodation' (p.137). This is a definition which includes young people who are actively seeking more secure accommodation even though they may be staying temporarily at another address, including being housed by relatives. Within the general population of homeless young people, however, research has highlighted a number of discrete areas of concern.

Youthfulness of homeless people

As Gill Jones suggests (1993) 'lack of good national British data makes it impossible to give an accurate figure for the current median age at leaving home' (p.40). The circumstances which surround those who leave home involuntarily or move into unstable accommodation make such evidence even more difficult to gather. Such research as has been conducted, therefore, has to be treated with an awareness of the impact which such difficulties may have produced upon its conduct and product. Nevertheless, evidence does exist to suggest that increasing numbers of 16 and 17 year olds have found themselves exposed to homelessness. Strathdee and Coster (1995) for example, reporting the results of survey of 635 new users of Centrepoint between the beginning of April and end of September 1995 found that,

> Since the late eighties the most marked trend in youth homelessness has been an increase in the number of young people aged 16 and 17 turning to agencies like Centrepoint for assistance. In 1987 16 and 17 year olds made up 40% of the newly homeless young people aged 16 to 19 admitted to Centrepoint's direct access shelters, by 1993/94 this had risen to 55% – a 38% increase.' (p.4)

Within the 16 and 17 year olds, moreover, the researchers found that 85 per cent of those interviewed reported having left their parental home as a result of being forced out by 'push factors', the highest proportion of any age group. Moreover, in the period of the survey, 'only 4% of young people who had left the parental home at 16 or 17 returned to their parents on leaving a Centrepoint hostel', confirming once again the extent to which homelessness is a matter of forced necessity, rather than choice, amongst this age group.

Young women

The caveats noted by Jones (1995) in relation to information concerning young people leaving home are repeated by writers who have considered the differential impact of gender upon the experience of young homelessness. Hutson and Liddiard (1994), for example, suggest that while there is some consensus that young women 'suffer disproportionately from homelessness...this is not always reflected in the homelessness statistics' (p.41). In their explanation, young women are under-represented in this way because such records as are available are generally collected by agencies whose provision is ill-suited to the needs of young women who therefore make little use of them. When more sensitive research enquiries are made, however, evidence of a different order begins to emerge. Within the Centre-point research, for example, Strathdee and Coster (1995) report that, 'women make up 53% of 16 and 17 year olds and 52% of the 16 and 17 year olds describe themselves as black or mixed race' (p.9). These findings concerning race and gender are borne out in other studies.

Further evidence of the over-representation of young women amongst this group comes from Anderson *et al.* (1993) for example, in their finding that 'the ratio of 16 and 17 year old homeless young women to men in their sample was 6 to 1.' This distribution of need is not reflected however, in the pattern of supply. Blair (1993), in a study of the allocation policies of housing associations found that nearly 90 per cent of associations did not have a policy for housing single women, 80 per cent did not consider women's housing needs in development policies and, where criteria were used to assess housing need these were less likely to include consideration of circumstances relevant to single women's housing needs.

Young black people

Over-representation of black young people amongst the young homeless has also been established over an extended period (see, e.g. in Smith and Gilford 1991). The most detailed and recent evidence comes from Davies *et al.* (1996) in their report of a year-long research project on youth homelessness amongst black and minority ethnic groups in England. The research draws on in-depth interviews with 126 young people in three areas, group discussions in two of those areas, and a survey of 88 agencies providing services to young homeless people. The study sets out its three main aims in the following way:

> to examine the extent of homelessness amongst young people from black and minority ethnic communities, to understand the ways in which homelessness is perceived and experienced by these people and the forms in which it is endured and to identify and document good practice in providing services for young black and minority ethnic single homeless people. (p.3)

Using the definition of homelessness outlined above, Davies *et al.* (1996) concluded that, 'evidence suggests that the numbers of young black and minority young ethnic single homeless people are rising disproportionate to their numbers per head of the population' (p.8). A profoundly disturbing proportion of young black homeless people – one in six of all respondents–reported *never* having had a place they could call home.

This study also emphasised the connection between accommodation problems and other social issues, with particular emphasis upon the absence of provision for those with mental health problems. From a social work perspective, the study reached a further significant conclusion:

> Young black people would appear less likely than their white counterparts to immediately turn to voluntary and statutory agencies for support when they become homeless. Young black single homeless people tend to turn to friends and other relations on becoming homeless and tend to stay in situ for long periods of time – thus accounting for the 'hidden homelessness' associated with this group. (p.8)

This finding was particularly acute in the case of young Asian homeless and, in the view of the researchers, pointed to two central conclusions – the need for ethnic diversity in service provision by statutory and voluntary agencies and the clear emergence of the overwhelming preference of African–Caribbean and Asian young people for what they perceive to be black-run hostels. 'There was absolutely no doubt as to the strength or unanimity of the feelings expressed on this issue and it is one of the most significant findings of the study' (p.89).

Homelessness and social work

A common theme in much of the research on youth homelessness is the extent to which the fate of young homeless people is linked to the availability (or otherwise) of quality services from adults. Many, of course, turn out already to have a history of involvement with social services organisations. Strathdee and Coster (1995) note that:

> Care leavers are disproportionately represented in the young people that Centrepoint sees. They are also more likely to be aged 16 and 17. 38% of the

16 and 17 year olds we see have been in care at some time compared to 23% of 18 to 25 year olds'. (p.15)

Davies *et al.* (1996) emphasise the extent to which success in overcoming homelessness is linked to the provision of 'much needed injection of staff resources and financial support...[without which] many young people are bound to fail at living independently' (p.86).

This chapter now turns to look directly at evidence of current practice within social service organisations in relation to young people, set against the general themes of youthful transition, contemporary social welfare practice and the extent of youth homelessness which have been explored above.

Statutory social work services for homeless young people are governed by two distinct streams of legislation: family and child welfare legislation on the one hand, and homeless legislation on the other. Currently these are primarily represented by the Children Act of 1989, which is administered through local authority Social Services Departments, and the Housing Act of 1985 which is implemented through council Housing Departments. A number of recent studies have considered the specific impact of this framework upon work with young homeless people, two of which are now considered below.

Kay (1994), approaching the issue of youth homelessness from the perspective of local authority housing departments, draws on a survey of such authorities' policies, including replies to a postal questionnaire from 293 authorities, with a response rate of 89 per cent. The purpose of the research was to study the ways in which homelessness authorities are interpreting their responsibilities to homeless 16 and 17 year olds, and how their policies and practices may have been affected by the 1989 Children Act and the perceived constraints which local authorities believe to have had an impact upon their ability to develop and provide services. The study begins by establishing the points of contact between the two pieces of legislation, contending that, 'There is a clear link between the Housing Act 1985 Part III and the Children Act 1989 in relation to homeless 16 and 17 year olds.' Amongst the sources cited in support of this contention was the judgement of Lord Justice Bingham who concluded in 1993 that:

Reading these two codes (to the legislation) side by side, I find a clear parliamentary intention that children in need should not fall between them. If children in need do not command protection under one code, they will

command it under the other. Sir Thomas Bingham M. R. in R B North Avon
DC ex parte Smith (1993) *The Times* 4 August 1993.

Against that background, the Kay study found that 71 per cent of housing authorities carried out assessments of all 16 and 17 year old homeless young people while 10 per cent did not and 18 per cent did so sometimes. Crucially, however, only 23 per cent of authorities

> accepted that homeless 16 and 17 year olds were vulnerable by virtue of age alone. The majority of housing authorities asked that young people fulfilled a range of other criteria before they were accepted as vulnerable under Part III of the Housing Act 1985. (p.2)

In practice, the linking criteria which led to a successful claim to vulnerability were almost always those which involved issues of health or likely public concern. These included mental health problems which 84 per cent of Departments regarded as proof of vulnerability, and pregnancy which was accepted by 92 per cent. The linking criteria which were significantly less successful in leading to an accepted claim to vulnerability were generally those which could be regarded as including some level of individual culpability such as a drug or alcohol problem which was accepted by only 42 per cent of Departments. Most strikingly, living on the streets was regarded as proof of vulnerability by only 27 per cent, while leaving care was regarded as meeting the definition by only half (52%) of Housing Departments.

To arrive at conclusions concerning responsibility to provide accommodation housing authorities normally undertook 'stringent assessment processes' in order to test claims to vulnerability. Evidence was required of local connection (83%), when claims were made to pregnancy (93%) and illness or disability (89%). Corroboration of evidence was also needed. Only 6 per cent of authorities 'said they would accept the young person's word in these circumstances' and 60 per cent said they required 'written evidence from doctors, social workers, lawyers or the police' before accepting evidence of vulnerability (p.3).

Local arrangements to resolve any tensions between Housing Act and Children Act responsibilities were by no means universal. Housing authorities reported undertaking formal negotiations with Social Services Departments in 60 per cent of cases, with informal discussion in a further 37 per cent. Yet, the outcome, according to the research was that 'less than a third of local housing associations had developed joint criteria with social services authorities on a mutual acceptance of "child in need" and "vulnerability"' (p.3). Indeed, from the standpoint of housing authorities, even this level of joint working was unattributable to the Children Act itself. Kay found that

> Only a quarter of housing authorities had changed their policy on vulnerability in relation to homeless 16 and 17 year olds since the intro- duction of the Children Act ..[while]....54% of housing authorities stated that the Children Act had not made any difference to the provision of services for young homeless people locally. (p.4)

The importance of a strategic approach to the resolution of these tensions has been emphasised in the recent research by Jacqui McCluskey (1997). A postal questionnaire for housing authorities in Wales and England, followed by in-depth interviews in a sample of these areas, revealed a picture in which authorities with a strategy have made much more positive progress – under the Children Act and the NHS and Community Care Act – for single homeless people, than those without a strategy.

Addressing the issue from the opposite side of the departmental and legal spectrum, Hoffman (1995) considered the discharge by Social Services Departments in Wales of their Children Act responsibilities towards homeless young people. The research, conducted for the housing charity Shelter, drew a 100 per cent response from the Departments. The author reaches conclusions which mirror some of those highlighted in the Kay study of housing authorities. Thus, while Hoffman (1995) concludes that 'the Children Act has....meant that youth homelessness is treated more seriously than perhaps was previously the case' (p.21), half the authorities in Wales continued to pursue a policy of not assisting all homeless 16 and 17 year olds on the basis of homelessness alone. In the words of the Report,

> the findings show that most social services departments exercise a two tier assessment procedure: one to establish 'child in need' which most homeless 16/17 year olds will come under, and another to establish whether the individual's welfare is going to be 'seriously prejudiced' without the provision of accommodation. Homelessness on its own does not establish entitlement to housing. (p.7)

In a damaging conclusion Hoffman contends that these decisions, rather than being the product of an assessment of a homeless young person's needs, are more often the product of resource constraint faced by social services departments: 'The evidence suggests that in many cases resource constraints are responsible for social services acting as 'gatekeepers' in the allocation of housing and support services, effectively excluding some young people and denying them their statutory rights.' The confusion of responsibility between housing and social services departments in relation to homeless young people added to these difficulties by allowing Children Act responsibilities to be evaded. The problem is set out by Hoffman (1995) as follows:

> the social services authority requests assistance from the housing authority in the discharge of their functions, having already established their duty to provide housing to a 'child in need'. Other authorities may in certain circumstances refuse to assist, but this should not adversely affect the right of a   young person to housing since *the refusal is a refusal to assist social services who continue to be obliged to house the young person.* This distinction is crucial yet not understood or acted upon by social services or other authorities. (p.11, emphasis added)

In Shelter's view this leads to a very particular conclusion: 'Social services departments should therefore seek to avoid referring young people to housing authorities'.

Conclusion

In this chapter we have attempted to address four core issues which we believe to be essential to any understanding of the links between young people and homelessness: the changing nature of the social contract between young people and society and the impact this has upon the transition from childhood to adulthood; the extent and nature of involvement by social workers in contact with individuals in these transitional years; the extent and nature of homelessness amongst young people; the particular responses of social welfare agencies to young people in that situation. We now aim to bring these themes together.

Homeless young people find themselves at a point where deficits and deterioration in a series of services all collide. In public policy, the elision from homelessness (which is 'voluntary') to begging (which is 'lucrative') to dangerousness (which is 'pervasive') to a vindictive response is one in which the only contest between the major political parties has been to appear more-punitive-than-thou. In social work, the shift to minimum intervention has left many young people with real needs without a source of help. Formulated during the very different social policy climate of the late 1970s, the limitations of such a practice approach have become increasingly exposed in a period when a real deterioration in young people's prospects has combined with cuts in services available to them. In housing provision, the effect of the Children Act upon the treatment of homeless young people has been variable, at the very best. Inadequately resourced itself, the Act attempts to impact upon a field of housing legislation which has, at the same time, been under continuous attack for being too generous and open to exploitation. Within such a discourse young people, particularly, in the shape of the demonised young-single-homeless-mother, emerge as part of the problem, rather than in need of a solution. The result, too often, is that local authorities continue to play one Act and one Department off against each other, with young people falling precipitately through the cracks which have been created.

Against such a bleak background, it would be misplaced to end this chapter with some spurious optimism about the future. Yet, even in these cheerless times, there are steps which could be taken by some players in the fields we have outlined. Without a very different approach by central government, there is little that can be expected from local housing authorities, or housing associations, by way of new provision for young homeless people. Instead, work has to continue at the margins, with new initiatives – such as the Foyer movement – or small scale and local projects (see Drakeford and Vanstone, 1996 for a number of examples of such projects within the youth justice field). Social work services, by contrast, have more to do in re-shaping and re-invigorating practice to meet the needs which young people now experience. In our prescription this means counteracting the burden of negativity which is projected upon young people in our society, moving beyond a narrow and defensive definition of Departmental responsibility in order to offer young people broader assistance in re-assembling the props of a sustaining lifestyle amongst the ruins of exhausted and desperate families and the assault upon their social rights. Re-engagement with the *social* dimension of young people's lives means moving beyond the minimum intervention preoccupation with avoiding harm, to a positive determination to do some good in the lives of those who depend upon social work services.

Social work by itself will not transform the picture which this chapter has unfolded. What it can do, however, is to maximise whatever opportunities can be found for young homeless people and act as a voice for those whose needs remain ignored or made worse by their treatment at the hands of adults. Of all the things which have happened to young homeless people in recent years, perhaps social work is most culpable in its failure to provide a voice for those young people who find it hardest to have their own voice heard. Recapturing that ground will not be easily accomplished or comfortably received, but if a better future for young homeless people is to be constructed then the debate needs to begin here.

References

Ainley, P. (1991) *Young People Leaving Home.* London: Cassell.

Anderson, I., Kemp, P. and Quilgars, D. (1993) *Single Homeless People.* London: Department of Environment.

Anderson, L. and Morgan, J. (1997) *Social Housing for Single People? A Study of Local Policy and Practice.* Stirling: Housing Policy and Practice Unit, Stirling University.

Blair, F. (1993) *Single Women in Housing Need: Improving Access to Housing Association Homes.* London: National Federation of Housing Associations.

Carnegie United Kingdom Trust (1997) *The Carnegie Young People Initiative: Years of Decision.* Leicester: Youth Work Press.

CHAR (1996) *We Didn't Choose to be Homeless* (UK Commission of Inquiry into Youth Homelessness). London: CHAR.

Coles, B. (1995) *Youth Citizenship and Young Careers.* London: UCL Press.

Collins, M. and Kelly, G. (1995) 'The relationship between care and justice.' *Child Care in Practice 2,* 2, 30-38.

Colton, M., Drury, C. and Williams, M. (1995) 'Evaluating family support services.' In M. Colton (ed) *The Art and Science of Child Care.* Aldershot: Arena.

Connelly J. and Crown, J. (eds) (1994) *Homelessness and Ill Health: Report of a Working Party of the Royal College of Physicians.* London: Royal College of Physicians.

Davies, J., Lyle, S., Deacon, A., Law, I., Julienne, L. and Kay H. (1996) *Discounted Vioces: Homelessness Amongst Young Black and Minority Ethnic People in England.* Departmental Working Party No 15, University of Leeds: School of Sociology and Social Policy.

Department of Health (1994) *Children Act Report.* London: HMSO.

Department of Health (1995) *Children and Young People on Child Protection Registers, year ending 31 March 1994, England.* London: HMSO.

Drakeford, M. and Vanstone, M. (eds) (1996) *Beyond Offending Behaviour.* Aldershot: Arena.

Haines, K. and Drakeford, M. (1997) *Youth Justice: A Handbook for Policy and Practice.* London: Macmillan.

Helve, H. and Bynner, J. (eds) (1996) *Youth and Life Management: Research Perspectives.* Helsinki: Helsinki University Press.

Hoffman, S. (1995) *The Children Act and Youth Homelessness in Wales.* Swansea: Shelter Cymru.

Home Office (1993) *Criminal Statistics, England and Wales 1992.* Cm 2410, London: HMSO.

Hutson, S. and Liddiard, M. (1994) *Youth Homelessness: The Construction of a Social Issue.* London: Macmillan.

Jones, G. (1995) *Leaving Home.* Buckingham: Open University Press.

Jones, G. and Wallace, C. (1992) *Youth, Family and Citizenship.* Buckingham: Open University Press.

Jones, R. (1984) 'Questioning the new orthodoxies.' *Community Care,* 11th October.

Kay, H. (1994) *Conflicting Priorities: Homeless 16 and 17 Year Olds: A Changing Agenda for Housing Authorities?* London: CHAR/Chartered Institute of Housing.

Kittrie, N. (1971) *The Right to be Different: Deviance and Enforced Therapy.* Baltimore: John Hopkins Press.

Leigh, C. (1994) *Everybody's Baby: Implementing Community Care for Single Homeless People.* London: CHAR.

McCluskey, J. (1993) *Reassessing Priorities, The Children Act 1989–A New Agenda for Young Homeless People?* London: CHAR.

McCluskey, J. (1994) *Acting in Isolation: An Evaluation of the Effectiveness of the Children Act for Young Homeless People.* London: CHAR.

McCluskey, J. (1997) *Where There's a Will...: Developing Single Homeless Strategies.* London: CHAR.

Morrow, V. and Richards, M. (1996) *Transitions to Adulthood: A Family Matter?* York: Joseph Rowntree Foundation.

NCH Action for Children (1995) *Factfile.* London: NCH Action for Children.

Pollitt, N., Booth, A. and Kay, H. (1989) *Hard Times: Young and Homeless.* London: Shelter.

Schur, E. (1971) *Labelling Deviant Behaviour.* New York: Harper and Row.

Smith, J. and Gilford, S. (1991) *Homelessness Among the Under-25s.* York: Joseph Rowntree Foundation.

Strathdee, R. (1992) *No Way Back: Homeless 16 and 17 Year Olds in the 90s.* London: Young Homeless Group.

Strathdee, R. (1993) *Housing Our Children.* London: Young Homelessness Group.

Strathdee, R. and Coster, D. (1995) *'They Don't Want Me Back': Benefit Changes and Homeless 16 and 17 Year Olds.* London: Young Homelessness Group.

Thorpe, D.H., Green, C. and Smith D. (1980) *Punishment and Welfare: Case Studies of the Workings of the 1969 Children and Young Persons Act.* Lancaster: Centre of Youth Crime and Community.

Welsh Office (1995) *Children and Young People on Child Protection Registers, Year Ending 31 March 1994, Wales.* Cardiff: HMSO.

Williamson, H. (1993) 'Youth policy in the United Kingdom and the marginalisation of young people.' *Youth and Policy 40,* 33–48.

Wilson, P. (1995) 'A mentally healthy young nation.' *Youth and Policy 51,* 60–63.

The Contributors

Chris Allen currently works as a Research Associate at the Centre for Housing Management and Development at the University of Wales, Cardiff. Prior to this he worked for the North Western Regional Association of Community Health Councils in Manchester. His substantive and theoretical research interests are the sociology of the body; the sociology of the emotions; the sociology of (medical, social work and housing) education and knowledge; representations and experiences of health, illness and disablement; comparative theories of divergence and multi country research methods; and the use and impact of methodological approaches to undertaking research with disabled people.

Mono Chakrabarti is Professor of Social Work at the University of Strathclyde in Glasgow. He is a qualified social worker and has studied at the University of Edinburgh and the London School of Economics. Before joining Strathclyde, he was a Lecturer in Social Work and Social Policy at the University of Glasgow. His research interests are migration and ethnicity, mental health, comparative social policy and vocational education. His publications have appeared in various academic journals and he has written a number of books.

David Clapham is Professor of Housing and Director of the Centre for Housing Management and Development at the University of Wales, Cardiff. His research interests include the role of housing in community care with a particular emphasis on housing and care for older people. Other interests include the social role of housing management and homelessness among young people. Among other publications, he is the author of *Housing and Social Policy* (Macmillan 1990) with Susan Smith and Peter Kemp.

Mark Drakeford is a lecturer in the School of Social and Administrative Studies at the University of Wales Cardiff. He has previously worked as a probation officer and a community development worker. His research interests include poverty, social welfare services and young people in general, and youth justice in particular.

Bridget Franklin is a lecturer in housing at Cardiff University of Wales and has previously held a number of research posts. Her research interests are in the housing implications of community care, the definition and role of housing management, and housing for disadvantaged and minority groups.

Jim Hayton is Head of Housing Development and Support Services at South Lanarkshire Council, prior to which he was Deputy Director of Housing at East Kilbride District

Council. He began his career with a community based housing association during which time he also served on the Council of the Scottish Federation of Housing Associations. He has an MPhil. in Housing Studies from Glasgow University.

Susan Lambert is a senior research assistant in the Department of Nursing, Midwifery and Health Care at University of Wales Swansea. She was previously a lecturer in social policy in the School of Social and Administrative Studies at University of Wales Cardiff. Her interests are in housing and health policy and gender issues.

Christine Oldman is a research fellow in the Centre for Housing Policy at the University of York, where she has worked since its creation in 1990. Before that she was research fellow in the Social Policy Research Unit at York. She has a long-standing interest in issues to do with housing and community care.

Ian Shaw is a senior lecturer and Director of Research in the School of Social and Administrative Studies at the University of Wales Cardiff. His research interests include evaluation, homelessness, prostitution, and the development of computer-assisted learning. He is the author of various books and research reports on these themes, and is extensively involved in the supported housing field.

Gill Stewart. As a senior lecturer in social work at Lancaster University, Gill Stewart has spent many years researching social workers' involvement with people who are poor and badly housed, and has published numerous books, research reports and articles on this subject. Previously she worked in a probation services team for homeless offenders and with various voluntary agencies in central London.

Fran Wasoff is a senior lecturer and head of department in the Department of Social Policy at Edinburgh University. Her interests are in gender and social policy, socio-legal studies and housing policy.

Howard Williamson is a Senior Research Associate in the School of Social and Administrative Studies, University of Wales Cardiff. He is also a practising youth worker and vice-chair of the Wales Youth Agency. He has researched and written widely on youth issues and has contributed to policy development at local, national and European levels. He is the author of *Children Speak* (with Ian Butler, Longman, 1994) and *Youth and Policy: Contexts and Consequences* (Ashgate 1997).

David Wiseman is Head of Strategic Services, South Lanarkshire Council, Social Work Services. He has worked with the social services, within Scotland, for over 24 years, first as a youth and community worker and then more recently in the strategic planning, regulation, contracting and quality assurance fields. David also spent nine years as an elected member of the City of Glasgow District Council, where for a period of time he was Chair of the Housing Committee.